STUDY FOR THE WORLD'S BODY

STUDY
FOR THE
WORLD'S BODY

new and
selected poems

DAVID ST. JOHN

HarperPerennial
A Division of HarperCollins*Publishers*

HarperCollins books may be purchased for educational, business, or sales promo-
tional use. For information please write: Special Markets Department, Harper-
Collins Publishers, Inc., 10 East 53rd Street, New York, NY 10022.

FIRST EDITION

Designed by Nancy Singer

LIBRARY OF CONGRESS CATALOGING-IN-PUBLICATION DATA
St. John, David, 1949–
    Study for the world's body : new and selected poems / David St. John.
—1st ed.
        p.   cm.
        ISBN 0-06-055349-9/ISBN 0-06-095016-1 (pbk.)
        I. Title.
PS3569.A4536S7 1994   93-47441
811'.54—dc20

94 95 96 97 98 ❖/HC 10 9 8 7 6 5 4 3 2 1
94 95 96 97 98 ❖/HC 10 9 8 7 6 5 4 3 2 1 (pbk.)

Acknowledgments

THE NEW POEMS IN THIS COLLECTION FIRST APPEARED IN THE FOLLOWING MAGAZINES:

The American Poetry Review: "My Friend" and "Study for the World's Body"

Antaeus: "I Know" and "Merlin"

Black Warrior Review: "Meditation"

Denver Quarterly: "Lucifer in Starlight" and "Los Angeles, 1954"

The New Virginia Review: "My Tea with Madame Descartes"

The Partisan Review: "Who Is She . . ."

Western Humanities Review: "A Fan Sketched with Silver Egrets"

OF THE SELECTED POEMS, THE FOLLOWING FIRST APPEARED IN:

Antaeus: "Slow Dance," "Song Without Forgiveness," "The Man in the Yellow Gloves," "The Day of the Sentry," and "Terraces of Rain"

The New Yorker: "Hush," "Iris," "Gin," "Dolls," "The Shore," "Blue Waves," "Guitar," "Hotel Sierra," "Until the Sea Is Dead," "The Swan at Sheffield Park," "Shadow," "Desire," "The Reef," and "Leap of Faith"

Poetry: "Elegy," "The Avenues," "The Boathouse," "Woman and Leopard," "No Heaven," and "The Doors"

"Last Night with Rafaella" appeared in *The Best American Poetry of 1990*

"Merlin" appeared in *The Best American Poetry of 1991*

"Lucifer in Starlight" appeared in *The Best American Poetry of 1992*

Contents

V. *Merlin:* New Poems

VI. *Coda*

STUDY FOR THE WORLD'S BODY

I. from *Hush*

Are we two or am I all alone

—Paul Éluard

Slow Dance

It's like the riddle Tolstoy
Put to his son, pacing off the long fields
Deepening in ice. Or the little song
Of Anna's heels, knocking
Through the cold ballroom. It's the relief
A rain enters in a diary, left open under the sky.
The night releases
Its stars, & the birds the new morning. It is an act of grace
& disgust. A gesture of light:
The lamp turned low in the window, the harvest
Fire across the far warp of the land. The somber
Cadence of boots returns. A village
Pocked with soldiers, the dishes rattling in the cupboard
As an old serving woman carries a huge, silver spoon
Into the room & as she polishes she holds it just
So in the light, & the fat
Of her jowls
Goes taut in the reflection. It's what shapes
The sag of those cheeks, & has
Nothing to do with death though it is as simple, & insistent.
Like a coat too tight at the shoulders, or a bedroom
Weary of its single guest. At last, a body
Is spent by sleep: A dream stealing the arms, the legs.
A lover who has left you
Walking constantly away, beyond that stand
Of bare, autumnal trees: Vague, & loose. Yet, it's only
The dirt that consoles the root. You must begin
Again to move, towards the icy sill. A small
Girl behind a hedge of snow
Working a stick puppet so furiously the passersby bump
Into one another, watching the stiff arms

Fling out to either side, & the nervous goose-step, the dances
Going on, & on
Though the girl is growing cold in her thin coat & silver
Leotard. She lays her cheek to the frozen bank
& lets the puppet sprawl upon her,
Across her face, & a single man is left twirling very
Slowly, until the street
Is empty of everything but snow. The snow
Falling, & the puppet. *That girl.* You close the window,
& for the night's affair slip on the gloves
Sewn of the delicate
Hides of mice. They are like the redemption
Of a drastic weather: Your boat
Put out too soon to sea,
Come back. Like the last testimony, & trace of desire. Or,
How your blouse considers your breasts,
How your lips preface your tongue, & how a man
Assigns a silence to his words. We know lovers who quarrel
At a party stay in the cool trajectory
Of the other's glance,
Spinning through pockets of conversation, sliding in & out
Of the little gaps between us all until they brush or stand at last
Back to back, & the one hooks
An ankle around the other's foot. Even the woman
Undressing to music on a stage & the man going home the longest
Way after a night of drinking remember
The brave lyric of a heel-&-toe. As we remember the young
Acolyte tipping
The flame to the farthest candle & turning
To the congregation, twirling his gold & white satin
Skirts so that everyone can see his woolen socks & rough shoes
Thick as the hunter's boots that disappear & rise
Again in the tall rice
Of the marsh. The dogs, the heavy musk of duck. How the leaves
Introduce us to the tree. How the tree signals
The season, & we begin
Once more to move: Place to place. Hand

4

To smoother & more lovely hand. A slow dance. To get along.
You toss your corsage onto the waters turning
Under the fountain, & walk back
To the haze of men & women, the lazy amber & pink lanterns
Where you will wait for nothing more than the slight gesture
Of a hand, asking
For this slow dance, & another thick & breathless night.
Yet, you want none of it. Only, to return
To the countryside. The fields & long grasses:
The scent of your son's hair, & his face
Against your side,
As the cattle knock against the walls of the barn
Like the awkward dancers in this room
You must leave, knowing the leaving as the casual
& careful betrayal of what comes
Too easily, but not without its cost, like an old white
Wine out of its bottle, or the pages
Sliding from a worn hymnal. At home, you walk
With your son under your arm, asking of his day, & how
It went, & he begins the story
How he balanced on the sheer hem of a rock, to pick that shock
Of aster nodding in the vase, in the hall. You pull him closer
& turn your back to any other life. You want
Only the peace of walking in the first light of morning,
As the petals of ice bunch one
Upon another at the lip of the iron pump & soon a whole blossom
Hangs above the trough, a crowd of children teasing it
With sticks until the pale neck snaps, & flakes spray everyone,
& everyone simply dances away.

Iris

Vivian St. John (1891–1974)

There is a train inside this iris:

You think I'm crazy, & like to say boyish
& outrageous things. No, there is

A train inside this iris.

It's a child's finger bearded in black banners.
A single window like a child's nail,

A darkened porthole lit by the white, angular face

Of an old woman, or perhaps the boy beside her in the stuffy,
Hot compartment. Her hair is silver, & sweeps

Back off her forehead, onto her cold & bruised shoulders.

The prairies fail along Chicago. Past the five
Lakes. Into the black woods of her New York; & as I bend

Close above the iris, I see the train

Drive deep into the damp heart of its stem, & the gravel
Of the garden path

Cracks under my feet as I walk this long corridor

Of elms, arched
Like the ceiling of a French railway pier where a boy

With pale curls holding

A fresh iris is waving goodbye to a grandmother, gazing
A long time

Into the flower, as if he were looking some great

Distance, or down an empty garden path & he believes a man
Is walking toward him, working

Dull shears in one hand; & now believe me: The train

Is gone. The old woman is dead, & the boy. The iris curls,
On its stalk, in the shade

Of those elms: Where something like the icy & bitter fragrance

In the wake of a woman who's just swept past you on her way
Home

& you remain.

Six/Nine/Forty-Four

Keith Douglas (1920–1944)

The black windows. Her arms,
pocked as the streets. The old man
drags a folding chair onto the fire escape,
to watch the sky. He says it's like the night
he gave up the marimbas for a woman
in an apricot gown dancing by the bandstand.
The air begins to swirl with a pink & white
dust of plaster & bricks. The old man
picks up his boater, & broken hand-mirror.
A sailor with no lashes, & a pearl
necklace, mimes
the moment his wife dipped their son's
foot into a bowl of tepid, sudsy water & all
hell blew apart & these quills of porcelain
into his face. Outside London,
a sleepy girl in a cakeshop is undisturbed
again by anything.
On a wedding cake, she repeats the two forks
of a road joining, lazy V's of lime & lemon icing.
She soft-shoes, & unties her apron. A long walk
home, & very late.

*

In North Africa, they
mark the crossroads with blank stones,
as if the stones were there first.
The chaplain's leading
services & a corporal playing
the hymns on a saxophone. The lizards,
& anise in the wind. At the camp's
edge, a wild dog rummages under canvas,
into the shallow graves. In Cairo,
his whore flips off a taxi driver & pukes,
& refuses tea. She says, Ice cream. A large man
in a white suit admires his own hands, & pours
his sherry into the blue rose on his table.
In Alamein, a censor dumps his scotch
over an orange sliced in a glass, & holds up
a poem typed on an aerogram, & can't decide.
He blacks the line about a Second Front,
& the rhyme of *tits* with *spits*,
& knows now it doesn't scan, but who gives
a fuck. Someone whose friend's
dressed in a greatcoat & a dog's face,
a friend leaning on his shoulder the long way
from Morocco to the Continent. Along the boat's
rail, & coughing. To a ragged
France, the slow clack of blood, & a soft,
black window in his gut. No poem, & drawings
in his pocket. A loosed bête noire. The third day
of Normandy. Keith Douglas.

*

The open window. Her arms,
pocked as the streets. The tea steeps
in the tin pot. Across the way, the theater
marquee flushes. She leans on the sill,
watching a sullen ticket girl press
her face against the faces
of a poster. She lays out the morphine
syrettes, & pours the tea, & puts a picture
of him in Cairo, a café's rag awning
shadowing his eyes, in a wood box by his poems.
As the newsreel begins, speeches & the applause
of guns drift over. The globe
of the radio's dial floats
out of its cabinet, a smoldering planet.
She turns the squat arrow like a deft & staunch
compass — Across the threads of line dividing
the world in a pie of vague hums, the endless
static of hymns, & days. A woman out
walking her dog
in a cemetery begins to laugh very loudly,
& uncontrollably. In the cherry orchards, the dead
branches, & stones the birds have left.

*

My father has fallen
asleep in the Shangri-La. The jukebox
sticks, & at the bar a blond bitches
ships & shipyards, the grease she scours
off her hands with kerosene. The bartender
polishes, & nods. She says her taste for fast
cars & martinis has gone.
A man kicks the jukebox, & my father lifts
his face off the cold table,
& straightens his flight jacket, & his cap.
He walks out into the glare of the California
afternoon; & like blood on the page
of your detective novel, or a rude drunk rising
like a bruise — I hold up 2 pictures. Look.
A fourth Xmas, at my father's feet. My face
a moon above the blue dark of a sailor's suit.
The blond curls like a pin-up girl's
across my forehead. Now this: the slick,
leather-shouldered pilots standing by the hard
wheels of a B–17. And these sons
putting their faces to pillows as cold
as a father's leather chest.
These sons picking through the silences
of abandoned Quonset huts, where they were born.
These fathers: suddenly air. Blown from cockpits
into the shrugs of sons, the shrugs of my friends
& poets; all of us walking out of these pages,
& the wars, & these fathers. I've fallen
asleep in the same Shangri-La.
Asleep in my father's old overcoat.

The woman beside me has a sour mouth, a sour
kiss. Poetry
deserves legacies. In France, it's nearly
afternoon, & I'm broke. Dead drunk. Very late,
& a long walk home.

Wedding Preparations
in the Country

This is a poem like a suitcase
Packed with flour. The baker eloping
With his lover insists on making his own wedding
Cake. Or, the mime in whiteface penciling his brows.
The white marble tombstone that Jude
Left blank, save
For the star more like a man's hand with the fingers
Spread than any star. In other words,
What is bleak is a table covered with snow, & the man
Beside it sipping coffee on his terrace
With a woman who is pale with anger pointing a pistol out
Across the blank, white lawn. Now the boy in whiteface
Delivers his bouquet: Cold lilies perhaps,
But more likely he tosses the limbs of a drama onto the terrace,
Or a few Chinese roses, & the promise of despair
Is as reliable as winter. As a suitcase spilling on the stairs.
The cake! Those squibs of icing,
Those stars squeezed from the nozzle of a paper cone
Onto these broad fields of cake.
The sorry stone admits that something's gone. Or someone.
Someone like you. Like the little man & woman riding
The cake. Close the suitcase. Go back down the snowy stairs.

Dolls

They are so like
Us, frozen in a bald passion
Or absent
Gaze, like the cows whose lashes
Sag beneath their frail sacks of ice.
Your eyes are white with fever, a long
Sickness. When you are asleep,
Dreaming of another country, the wheat's
Pale surface sliding
In the wind, you are walking in every breath
Away from me. I gave you a stone doll,
Its face a dry apple, wizened, yet untroubled.
It taught us the arrogance of silence,
How stone and God reward us, how dolls give us
Nothing. Look at your cane,
Look how even the touch that wears it away
Draws up a shine, as the handle
Gives to the hand. As a girl, you boiled
Your dolls, to keep them clean, presentable;
You'd stir them in enormous pots,
As the arms and legs bent to those incredible
Postures you preferred, not that ordinary, human
Pose. How would you like me? —
Leaning back, reading aloud from a delirious
Book. Or sprawled across your bed,
As if I'd been tossed off a high building
Into the street,
A lesson from a young government to its people.
When you are asleep, walking the fields of another

Country, a series of shadows slowly falling
Away, marking a way,
The sky leaning like a curious girl above a new
Sister, your face a doll's deliberate
Ache of white, you walk along that grove of madness,
Where your mother waits. Hungry, very still.
When you are asleep, dreaming of another country,
This is the country.

Gin

There's a mystery
By the river, in one of the cabins
Shuttered with planks, its lock
Twisted; a bunch of magazines flipped open,
A body. A blanket stuffed with leaves
Or lengths of rope, an empty gin bottle.
Put down your newspaper. Look out
Beyond the bluffs, a coal barge is passing,
Its deck nearly
Level with the water, where it comes back riding
High. You start talking about nothing,
Or that famous party, where you went dressed
As a river. They listen,
The man beside you touching his odd face
In the countertop, the woman stirring tonic
In your glass. Down the bar the talk's divorce,
The docks, the nets
Filling with branches and sour fish. Listen,
I knew a woman who'd poke a hole in an egg, suck
It clean and fill the shell with gin,
Then walk around all day disgusting people
Until she was so drunk
The globe of gin broke in her hand. She'd stay
Alone at night on the boat, come back
Looking for another egg. That appeals to you, rocking
For hours carving at a hollow stone. Or finding
A trail by accident, walking the bluff's
Face. You know, your friends complain. They say
You give up only the vaguest news, and give a bakery

As your phone. Even your stories
Have no point, just lots of detail: The room
Was long and bright, small and close, angering Gaston;
They turned away to embrace him; She wore
The color out of season,
She wore hardly anything at all; Nobody died; Saturday.
These disguises of omission. Like forgetting
To say obtuse when you talk about the sun, leaving
Off the buttons as you're sewing up the coat. So,
People take the little
They know to make a marvelous stew;
Sometimes, it even resembles you. It's not so much
You cover your tracks, as that they bloom
In such false directions. This way friends who awaken
At night, beside you, awaken alone.

Hush

for my son

The way a tired Chippewa woman
Who's lost a child gathers up black feathers,
Black quills & leaves
That she wraps & swaddles in a little bale, a shag
Cocoon she carries with her & speaks to always
As if it were the child,
Until she knows the soul has grown fat & clever,
That the child can find its own way at last;
Well, I go everywhere
Picking the dust out of the dust, scraping the breezes
Up off the floor, & gather them into a doll
Of you, to touch at the nape of the neck, to slip
Under my shirt like a rag — the way
Another man's wallet rides above his heart. As you
Cry out, as if calling to a father you conjure
In the paling light, the voice rises, instead, in me.
Nothing stops it, the crying. Not the clove of moon,
Not the woman raking my back with her words. Our letters
Close. Sometimes, you ask
About the world; sometimes, I answer back. Nights
Return you to me for a while, as sleep returns sleep
To a landscape ravaged
& familiar. The dark watermark of your absence, a hush.

II. from *The Shore*

*We might hurt each other if we were
together; but apart, we should be hurt
much more and to less purpose.*

—Sidney Keyes,
in a letter

The Shore

So the tide forgets, as morning
Grows too far delivered, as the bowls
Of rock and wood run dry.
What is left seems pearled and lit,
As those cases
Of the museum stood lit
With milk jade, rows of opaque vases
Streaked with orange and yellow smoke.
You found a lavender boat, a single
Figure poling upstream, baskets
Of pale fish wedged between his legs.
Today, the debris of winter
Stands stacked against the walls,
The coils of kelp lie scattered
Across the floor. The oil fire
Smokes. You turn down the lantern
Hung on its nail. Outside,
The boats aligned like sentinels.
Here beside the blue depot, walking
The pier, you can see the way
The shore
Approximates the dream, how distances
Repeat their deaths
Above these tables and panes of water —
As climbing the hills above
The harbor, up to the lupine drifting
Among the lichen–masked pines,
The night is pocked with lamps lit
On every boat offshore,
Galleries of floating stars. Below,

On its narrow tracks shelved
Into the cliff's face,
The train begins its slide down
To the warehouses by the harbor. Loaded
With diesel, coal, paychecks, whiskey,
Bedsheets, slabs of ice — for the fish,
For the men. You lean on my arm,
As once
I watched you lean at the window;
The bookstalls below stretched a mile
To the quay, the afternoon crowd
Picking over the novels and histories.
You walked out as you walked out last
Night, onto the stone porch. Dusk
Reddened the walls, the winds sliced
Off the reefs. The vines of the gourds
Shook on their lattice. You talked
About that night you stood
Behind the black pane of the French
Window, watching my father read some long
Passage
Of a famous voyager's book. You hated
That voice filling the room,
Its light. So tonight we make a soft
Parenthesis upon the sand's black bed.
In that dream we share, there is
One shore, where we look out upon nothing
And the sea our whole lives;
Until turning from those waves, we find
One shore, where we look out upon nothing
And the earth our whole lives.
Where what is left between shore and sky
Is traced in the vague wake of
(The stars, the sandpipers whistling)
What we forgive. *If you wake soon, wake me.*

Blue Waves

I think sometimes
I am afraid, walking out with you
Into the redwoods by the bay. Over
Cioppino in a fisherman's café, we
Talk about the past, the time
You left me nothing but your rugs;
How I went off to that cabin
High in the Pacific cliffs — overlooking
Coves, a driftwood beach, sea otters.
Some mornings, over coffee, we sit
And watch the sun break between factory
Smokestacks. It is cold,
Only the birds and diesels are starting
To sound. When we are alone
In this equation of pleasure and light,
The day waking, I remember more
Plainly those nights you left a husband,
And I a son. Still, as the clouds
Search their aqua and grey
Skies, I want only to watch you leaning
Back in the cane chair, the Navaho
Blanket slipping, the red falls
Of your hair rocking as you keep time
To the machinery gears, buses
Braking to a slide, a shudder of trains.
If I remember you framed by an
Open window, considering the coleus
You've drawn; or, with your four or five
Beliefs, stubborn and angry, shoving
Me out the door of the Chevy; or, if some

Day or night
You take that suitcase packed under
The bed and leave once again, I will look
Back across this room, as I look now, to you
Holding a thin flame to the furnace,
The gasp of heat rising as you rise;
To these mornings, islands —
The balance of the promise with what lasts.

The Avenues

Some nights when you're off
Painting in your studio above the laundromat,
I get bored about two or three A.M.
And go out walking down one of the avenues
Until I can see along some desolate side street
The glare of an all-night cafeteria.
I sit at the counter,
In front of those glass racks with the long,
Narrow mirrors tilted above them like every
French bedroom you've ever read
About. I stare at all those lonely pies,
Homely wedges lifted
From their moons. The charred crusts and limp
Meringues reflected so shamelessly —
Their shapely fruits and creams all spilling
From the flat pyramids, the isosceles spokes
Of dough. This late at night,
So few souls left
In the place, even the cheesecake
Looks a little blue. With my sour coffee,
I wander back out, past a sullen boy
In leather beneath the whining neon,
Along those streets we used to walk at night,
Those endless shops of spells: the love philtres
And lotions, 20th century voodoo. Once,
Over your bath, I poured
One called *Mystery of the Spies*,
Orange powders sizzling all around your hips.

Tonight, I'll drink alone as these streets haze
To a pale grey. I know you're out somewhere —
Walking the avenues, shadowboxing the rising
Smoke as the trucks leave their alleys and loading
Chutes — looking for breakfast, or a little peace.

Guitar

I have always loved the word *guitar*.

I have no memories of my father on the patio
At dusk, strumming a Spanish tune,
Or my mother draped in that fawn wicker chair
Polishing her flute;
I have no memories of your song, distant Sister
Heart, of those steel strings sliding
All night through the speaker of the car radio
Between Tucumcari and Oklahoma City, Oklahoma.
Though I've never believed those stories
Of gypsy cascades, stolen horses, castanets,
And stars, of Airstream trailers and good fortune,
Though I never met Charlie Christian, though
I've danced the floors of cold longshoremen's halls,
Though I've waited with the overcoats at the rear
Of concerts for lute, mandolin, and two guitars —
More than the music I love scaling its woven
Stairways, more than the swirling chocolate of wood

I have always loved the word *guitar*.

Elegy

If there is any dwelling place
  for the spirits of the just;
if, as the wise believe, noble souls
  do not perish with the body,
rest thou in peace . . .

—Tacitus

Who keeps the owl's breath? Whose eyes desire?
Why do the stars rhyme? Where does
The flush cargo sail? Why does the daybook close?

So sleep and do not sleep.

The opaque stroke lost across the mirror,
The clamp turned.
The polished nails begin the curl into your palms.
The opal hammock of rain falls out of its cloud.

I name you, *Gloat-of-*
The-stalks, drowse-my-embers, old-lily-bum.
No matter how well a man sucks praise in the end
He sucks earth. Go ahead, step
Out into that promised, rasp gratitude of night.

Seeds and nerves. *Seeds*

And nerves. I'll be waiting for you, in some
Obscure and clarifying light;
I will say, Look, there is a ghost ice on the land.

If the page of marble bleeds in the yellow grass,
If the moon–charts glow useless and cold,

If the grains of the lamp outlast you, as they must —
As the tide of black gloss, the marls, and nectar rise

I will understand.

Here are my gifts: *smudges of bud,*
A blame of lime. Everything you remember crowds
Away. Stubble memory,
The wallpaper peeling its leaves. Fog. Fog
In the attic; this pod of black milk. Anymore,

Only a road like August approaches.

Sometimes the drawers of the earth close;
Sometimes our stories keep on and on. So listen —

Leave no address. Fold your clothes into a little
Island. Kiss the hinges goodbye. Sand the fire. Bitch
About *time.* Hymn away this reliquary fever.

How the sun stands crossing itself in the cut glass.

How the jonquils and bare orchards fill each morning
In mist. The branches in the distance stiffen,
Again. The city of stars pales.
In my fires the cinders rise like black angels;
The trunks of the olives twist once towards the world.

Once. I will walk out into the day.

The Boathouse

All the last lessons of fatigue,
Every passage naming its reprieve —
Also, the few
Commitments of the heart. I thought
I'd pass as smoothly as a hand passes
Over a globe of light
Hanging in some roadside bar,
Or over the earth on its pedestal of oak
In a library. I believed I'd take
What came, a life with no diary's
Hieroglyphics,
Only the crooked arc of the sun.
Now, even the way I sleep speaks habit;
My body slipping into the heat,
The crumpled beds. Every voice I hear
Within my own (*of the father,*
The mother) remains a saying so
Lost to its history. Look
How I treated the day,
Waking listlessly beyond the pale
Of those horizons scored along another
Subtle back. And so trust
Seeps only into the most concrete
And simple acts: the fox coat, the slap,
The gin smashed against the window. Maybe
Homer had it right. A man sails
The long way home. Now,
Every new morning-after lights
Those medleyed veins of white wisteria

Strung
Above the door; no alibis survive. Half
Of the boathouse has collapsed, the shingled
Roof sloughing off its tiles — as
Even the sea sings one octave in the past.

Hotel Sierra

The November air
Has curled the new leaves
Of the spider plant, strung
From an L-bent nail
Driven in the warp of the window
Frame. Maybe the woman down
At the desk has a few more opinions —
On the dying plant, or the high
Bruised clouds of the nearing storm,
Or the best road
Along the coast this time of year
To Oregon. This morning, after
You left to photograph
The tide pools at dawn, the waves
In their black–and–white
Froth, I scavenged in your bag
For books, then picked up one
You'd thrown onto the bed, Cocteau,
Your place marked with a snapshot
Of a whale leaping clear of the spray
Tossed by the migrating
Herd — a totem
Of what you've left to dream. Yet,
It's why we've come — *Hotel Sierra* —
To this place without a past for us,
Where, I admit, a dozen years ago
I stayed a night across
The hall. I never asked why, on this
Ocean, a hotel was named for mountains
Miles inland. I spent that cold

Evening playing pinball in some dank
Arcade. Tonight, I'll take you there,
Down by the marina with no sailboats,
By the cannery's half-dozing, crippled
Piers rocking in the high tides and winds
Where I sat out on the rotted boards,
The fog barely sifting down,
The few lights
Looped over those thin, uneasy poles
Throbbing as the current came and went.
Soon, I could see only two mast lights
Blinking more and more faintly
Towards the horizon. I took
A flask of gin upstairs, just to sit
At the narrow window drinking
Until those low-slung, purposeful
Boats returned. As I
Wait here this morning, for you,
For some fragment of a final scene,
I remember how I made you touch, last
Night in the dark, those
Summer moths embossed upon the faded,
Imperial wallpaper of the room.
Now, as I watch you coming up
The brick-and-stone path to the hotel,
I can hear those loose wood shutters
Of the roof straining in the winds
As the storm closes
Over the shore. I listen as you climb
The stairs, the Nikon buzzing
Like a smoked hive
Each moment as you stop in front of:
A stair step; a knob of the banister;
The worn brass "12" nailed
To our door; the ribbons: knots of paint

Peeling off the hall —
You knock open the door with one boot,
Poised, clicking off shot after
Shot as you slide into the cluttered room,
Pivoting: *me; the dull seascape hung*
Above the bed; the Bible I'd tossed
Into the sink; my hands curled on
The chair's arm; the limp spider plant. . . .
Next week, as you step out
Of the darkroom with the glossy proofs,
Those strips of tiny tableaux, the day
And we
Will have become only a few gestures
Placed out of time. But now rain
Slants beyond a black sky, the windows
Tint, opaque with reflected light;
Yet no memory is stilled, held frame
By frame, of this burlesque of you
Undressing. The odd pirouette
As your sweater comes off, at last,
Rain-soaked slacks collapsing on the floor.
Tomorrow, after we leave for good
The long story we've told of each other
So many years not a friend believes it,
After we drive along the shore to Albion
To your cabin set high above the road,
After we drag your suitcases and few boxes
Up to the redwood porch,
After the list of goodbyes and refusals ends,
We'll have nothing to promise. Before I go,
You'll describe for me again those sleek
Whales you love, the way they arc elegantly
Through water or your dreams. How, like
Us, they must travel in their own time,
Drawn simply by the seasons, by their lives.

Song Without Forgiveness

You should have known. The moon
Is very slender in that city. If those
Letters I sent,
Later, filled with details of place
Or weather, specific friends, lies, hotels —
It is because I took the attitudes of
Shadow for solitude. It is because you swore
Faith stands upon a black or white square,
That the next move
Is both logical and fixed. Now, no shade
Of memory wakes where the hand upon a breast
Describes the arc of a song without forgiveness.
Everything is left for you. After the bitter
Fields you walk grow deep with sweet weeds, as
Everything you love loves nothing yet,
You will remember, days, you should have known.

Until the Sea Is Dead

What the night prepares,
Day gives: this cool
Green weave to the light
Shading the darker emeralds
Of each branch as they descend
The narrow trunks of pine
And Douglas fir along the steep
Uneven slope of the hill,
Its jagged sockets of rock
And sudden gullies. Every amber
Bridge light fades at dawn,
A few redwoods cluster
By the pitted highway
At each bend, and, beyond,
Those white hummocks rise shagged
With ice plant and wiry scrub
Half a mile or so
Before they flatten at the sea.
There the shore cuts like a thin
Sickle at the fields
Of black waves. On a rise above
These dunes, I watch the wild oats
Leaning with the wind, as I try
To imagine what I could
Write to you beyond these few
Details of a scene, or promises
You already know. Perhaps
I'll draw myself into the landscape,
To hold you closer to it

Than I could alone. Below, the dunes
Grow dark even in this harsh
A light: the sand burns
With the same erratic white
Within a negative held up
Against the sun. These dunes —
The Dunes of Abraham — were named
For the story of a Russian
Trader who stayed
To live in the hills above Fort Ross,
Long after his fur company
And its hundred soldiers sailed home
To Alaska. In the spring
His Spanish wife left him, leaving
Also the clothes and books brought
From Madrid, and her small son,
Almost two. Late one night, he took
The boy down to the dunes
And tied him against the bent
Skeleton of an overturned skiff;
In the moonlight, the child
Shone blue and flat, like the fresco
Of a cherub painted high
Across the dome of a cathedral ceiling.
The Russian took his curved fishing
Knife, then hooked
Its point into the skin below
His chin's cleft and yanked the blade
Along the fraying vein of his
Own windpipe. At dawn, a woman driving
A drag of timbers
From the mill down to the harbor
Found the boy, alive, his skin laced
By welts where the taut ropes

Webbed his body. In towns along
The coast, they said
It was a miracle the way God
Had turned the hand of Abraham away
From the son, against the father. Some
Nights, in the pockets of these dunes,
A gull or bat will sweep up
In an ashen light, startled by the whisk
Of my pants in the stiff grass;
I'll stop until the urgent flapping
Dies, until both the body
And its shadow enter the fog beginning
Its nightly burning of the shore.
As the horns sound, a beacon
From the jetty skims the vague sands
Of the reefs. From here,
I can see the husk of the De Soto
Someone pushed, last summer, off the cliff.
If I'm tired, sometimes
I'll sit awhile in its back seat —
In the mixed scent of salt, dead mollusks,
Moldering leather, and rust. The rear axle
Caught on the last low rocks
Of the cliff, the hood nosed dead–on
Into the tentative waves of a high tide,
The odd angle of the car,
Make it seem at any moment the rocks
Might give way, sending me adrift.
And I know I'll bring you here,
If only to let you
Face those dreams you woke me from
One night as the shore broke; I want
You to stand *here* —
Or, if you're bored with me,

We can walk up to the Whalers' Cove
Where a few old shacks are left
By a single room–sized caldron
Blackened by its years
Of fires melting acres of fat,
A pot too huge for even the scavengers
To think of carting it away. A local
Fisherman told me it was here
The Russian and his wife
Traded those first hard vows
Made to last longer than a double
Lifetime. Some
Should know better than to promise
Time, or their bodies, even if
Trust lives first in the body
Before rising like an ether
Into the mind. Tonight, waking alone,
I'll walk out into the cold mists
Up to the circular groves
High above the cabin, where the wild
Peacocks primp by the meadows or cry
From their invisible balconies
In the trees, their screams
Those of a child. And
From a prospect
Higher still, where the trees
Begin to grow more sparse and the rocks
More bare, I can look down
Onto the whole of the small harbor,
The bridge lights swaying
Once again, the jetty warning lamps
Blinking along the tower of the unlit
Beacon. The dunes rise and fall
Like shadows of waves down to the bay.

If you had been beside me, sleepless
Or chilled by the sudden violence
Of the winds, maybe you'd have walked
Here with me, or come after
To see what kept me standing in the night —
You'd see nothing. Only, what
Dissolves: dark to dawn, shore to wave,
Wings to fog, a branch to light:
The vague design that doesn't come
From me, yet holds me
To it, just as you might, another time.
And just as the Russian paced here
Rehearsing these lines, looking
Down onto the cove and whalers' shacks
Where she waited drawing a black
Comb out of her hair, I'll
Say for both of us the small prayer
Sworn to live beyond the night:
Until the stars run to milk,
Until the earth divides, until these waves
No longer rake the headland sands,
Until the sea is dead. . . .

III. from *No Heaven*

Winter Fires

There are lights soft as milk striking
Across the large distant delay
The mistakes the mission the act are all
One with the evening
                              If any *furthermore*
Still resides in the memory of reeds
Fired beneath the stoked dead limbs of pine
It is only the simple word of it
That future you gave

I will not remain in the remote grain
Of shadow rubbed over
The backdrop of rain *for miles* the rain
Neither will I go forgetting you never
Never even like the cold

I will stand like a flame in the flame

When the frost sears the brass of
The staircase
                    when the heart of shale
Ticks away in the tall cedar clock
Flecks & seconds passing   *passing*
I will stand very still in your absence

Where the shape of the shame has been named

The Day of the Sentry

Misery etcetera
Likely as the quilt of leaves
Above this confused congruence of
Sentience

If there were only one path leading away

From the small iron shed
Beside the glass summerhouse where
She sleeps like the broken string of a lute
Like the last in a series of broken
Strings

I might follow that path to the edge
Of the white lake the radical lake rising
All by itself onto the air

Where a single cloud descended like a hand

Once while we sat watching
As the moon paced the hard horizon like a sentry
Whose borders had only recently begun
To assemble
Whose latitudes resemble a doubled thread
Whose path remains a sentence on the sleepy tongue

& in that mist of intersection
Lake cloud & moon combining in the slash
Of the instant

I had only the physical to remember you by

Only the heat of your breath along my shoulder
Only the lit web of wet hair streaking
Our faces like the veins of
No other night

No other
Now in the regrettable glare of the mind

Which worships our impermanence
The way in which you have become the *she* asleep
In the summerhouse
                    where the glass walls
Hold only the gold of the day's light

As if you never had any body I knew at all

A Hard & Noble Patience

There is a hard & noble patience
I admire in my friends who are dead
Though I admit there are none of them
I would change places with

For one thing look how poorly they dress

Only one is still beautiful
& that is because
She chose to drown herself in a Swiss lake
Fed by a glacier said in local myth
To be a pool of the gods

& when her body was found she was so
Preserved by the icy currents
That even her eyelashes seemed to quiver
Beneath my breath

Though that was only for an instant

Before she was strapped to a canvas stretcher
& loaded into a blue van
Soon I was the only person still standing
At the lake's edge   A man made lonely
By such beauty

A man with less than perfect faith in any God

The Lemons

The white villa sat at the lip of rock
Like a slab of ice above the jade
Water & from the village
Across the harbor it seemed to ripple
In the waves of heat rising off the day

He was asleep in the wicker chaise
He'd pulled to the far edge
Of the stone veranda
Dressed in nothing except a black bikini
Suntan oils & a gold link chain
Around his wrist

Unconsciously with one hand he was cupping
His genitals & with the other in his
Sleep swatting flies

She put down the white coffee cup
& walked into the bedroom
Taking from the bottom drawer of the oak
Dresser the small black Beretta
Then she stepped out onto the terrace
Facing away from the sea where the lemon trees
Rose on the near hillside & took aim
At a sequence of possibilities

& on the veranda above the sea
He awoke to the irregular popping of the gun
Echoing through the rooms of the villa

& as he stood up unsteadily
Blinking for a moment in the white glare
He glanced up at the sky & knew
That soon he would be hearing the symphony
Of pans as the cook began the late-afternoon meal

Of rancor & fried eels

Desire

There is a small wrought-iron balcony . . .
& at that balcony she stood a moment
Watching a summer fog
Swirl off the river in huge
Drifting pockets as the street lights grew
Alternately muted then wild then to a blurred
Relay of yellow

Her hair was so blond that from a distance
It shone white as spun silk
& as he turned the corner he stopped suddenly
Looking up at the window of the hotel room
Where she stood in her Japanese kimono
Printed with red dragonflies
& a simple bridge

& in that lapse of breath
As the fog both offered & erased her in the night
He could remember every pulse of her tongue
Every pared detail of constancy left
Only to them   as he began
Walking slowly toward the door of the hotel
Carrying the hard loaf of day-old bread
& plums wrapped in newspaper

Already remembering this past he would desire

Woman and Leopard

Jardin des Plantes; the zoo.

Although she was beautiful,
Although her black hair, clipped
Just at the shoulders, glistened
Like obsidian as she moved
With that same slow combination
Of muscles as a dancer stepping
Casually beyond the spotlight
Into the staged, smoky
Blue of the shadows, it was
None of this that bothered me,
That made me follow her as she
Walked with her friends — a couple
Her age — along the wide dirt path
Leading to the island, the circle
Of cages where the cats glared
And paced. She was wearing a leather
Jacket, a simple jacket, cut narrowly
At the waist and dyed a green
I'd always coveted both in
Nature and out. It was the green of
Decay, of earth, of bronze covered by
The fine silt of the city, the green
Of mulch, of vines at the point
Of the most remote depth
In one of Rousseau's familiar jungles;
It was that jacket I was following —
Its epaulets were torn at the shoulders;
The back was crossed by swatches
Of paler, worn horizons
Rubbed away by the backs of chairs;

Along the arms, the scars of cigarettes
And knives, barbed wire . . .
I think it was she who nailed that poster
To the wall of my small room in
The Hôtel des Écoles, an ancient photo
Of the Communards marching in a phalanx
Toward the photographer, tools
And sticks the poor
Weapons held ready in their hands.
It was a poster left up by every
Student or transient spending a night
Or week in that for-real garret,
Its one window opening out
Onto the roof, letting in both
The sunlight and winter rains, the drops
Or streams from the laundry hung to dry
At the window ledge, all of it
Running down along the poster, leaving
Streaks as ocher as the rivers crossing
The map of Europe pinned to the opposite
Wall. On the poster, faded by
Every year, those at the edge of the march
Had grown more and more ghostly, slowly
Evaporating into the sepia: half men,
Half women, half shadow. And I think
It was she in that leather jacket closing
The door to this room in May 1968 to march
With all the other students to the Renault
Factory, to plead again for some
Last unity. Those scars along the arms
Were neatly sutured in that heavy
Coarse thread that sailors use, a thread
Of the same fecund green. The woman,
Thirty-five perhaps, no more, glanced
At me; I watched

As she moved off away from her friends,
Over to the waist-high, horizontal
Steel rail at the front of the leopard's
Cage. I moved to one side, to see both
Her face and the face
Of the leopard she'd chosen to watch;
She began to lock it into her precise,
Cool stare. The leopard sat on
A pillar of rock
Standing between the high metal walkway
At the rear of the cage, where its mate
Strolled lackadaisically, and — below
The leopard — a small pond that stretched
Almost to the cage's front, a pool
Striped blue-and-black by the thin shadows
Of the bars. The woman stood
Very quietly, leaning forward against
The cold steel of the restraint, the rail
Pressing against the bones
Of her hips,
Her hands balled in the pockets
Of her jacket. She kept her eyes on the eyes
Of the leopard . . . ignoring the chatter of
Her friends, of the monkeys, of the macaws.
She cared just for the leopard,
The leopard tensing and arching his back
As each fork of bone pushed up
Along its spine — just
For the leopard
Working its claws along its high perch
Of stone, its liquid jade eyes
Dilating, flashing only for an instant
As the woman suddenly laughed,
And it leapt.

Shadow

I am the shadow you once blessed

Though I was told later you meant only
To bless a small monkey carved of ebony
On the leg of a particular chair

Didn't you notice
That when you fell to your knees I too
Fell & kissed this scarlet earth

Blackened by the lyre of your wings

Meridian

The day seemed suddenly to give to black-&-white
The falcon tearing at the glove
Clare yanking down the hood over its banked eyes
& handing the bird
Its body still rippling & shuddering & flecked
Here or there with blood
                              to her son Louis
& as we walked back up the overgrown stone trail
To the castle now in the public trust
For tax reasons she admitted
Supposing one more turn in the grave couldn't harm
Her father the Count much at this point anyway
Though she flew his favorite red flag
From one of the towers every year
To mark each anniversary of his death
& though her beauty had acquired the sunken
Sheen of a ship's figurehead lifted
From the clear Mediterranean
As she walked ahead of me in her high chocolate boots
I could think only of her body still muscled like a
Snake's & how she lay sprawled last night
Naked on the blue tiles of the bathroom floor
& as I stepped into the doorway
I could see the bathtub speckled with vomit
The syringe still hanging limply from a vein in her
Thigh & she was swearing
As she grasped for the glass vial
That had rolled out of reach behind the toilet
Then she had it

Drawing herself up slowly as she
Turned her body slightly to look up at me
& she said nothing
Simply waiting until I turned & walked away
The door closing with its soft collapse
Behind me
                now over lunch on the terrace
I pin a small sprig of parsley to her jacket lapel
A kind of truce   a soldier's decoration
& above us the sun drags the day toward its meridian
Of heat & red wine & circumstance from which
We can neither look back nor step ever
Visibly beyond yet as we
Look at each other in the brash eclipsing glare
We know what bridging silence to respect
Now that neither of us has the heart to care

Interlude: Hephaestion's Prayer

Because I love you more than any

Forgive me now for leaving you
But please understand how tired I am
This evening
> *how thirsty & how cold*

& though I know it is only the fever
I still wish in my nightmares

I was simply the wind

Then I could speak to you forever after
Whenever the black leaves shook

Because I love you more than any
Please understand I will be as lonely
In whatever place the fever or
The gods will take me

& even if it is not home

Please swear to me
Because you love me more than any

You will not try to follow

Wavelength

They were sitting on the thin mattress
He'd once rolled & carried up the four floors
To his room only to find it covered nearly all
Of the bare wood
Leaving just a small path alongside the wall

& between them was the sack
Of oranges & pears she'd brought its neck
Turned back to expose the colors of the fruit
& as she opened a bottle of wine
He reached over to a tall stack of books
& pulled out *The Tao* & with a silly flourish
Handed it across the bed to her   she looked up
& simply poured the two squat water glasses
Half-full with wine & then she
Took the book   reading silently   not aloud
As he'd assumed & suddenly he felt clearly
She knew the way
Two people must come upon such an understanding
Together of course but separately
As the moon & the wave remain individually one

The Reef

The most graceful of misunderstandings
I could not keep close at hand
She paused a moment
At the door as she adjusted her scarf against
The winds & sprays & in the moonlight
She rowed back across the inlet to the shore

I sat alone above my pale vodka
Watching its smoky trails of peppercorns
Rising toward my lips

& while I flicked the radio dial
Trying to pick up the Cuban station or even
The static of "The Reggae Rooster" from Jamaica

I watched the waves foam above the coral & recede

Then foam breathlessly again & again
As a school of yellowtail
Rose together to the surface & then suddenly dove
Touched I knew by the long silver glove

Of the barracuda she loved to watch each afternoon
As she let the boat drift in its endlessly

Widening & broken arc

The Swan at Sheffield Park

It is a dim April
Though perhaps no dimmer than any
London April my friend says
As we turn our backs
To the crooked Thames to the stark
London skyline
                   walking up the hill's
Mild slope to one of the paths
And prospects of Kew
He introduces
The various and gathered families
Of trees then every subtle
Shift of design along the grounds
The carefully laid views and pools
The chapel-sized orangery
Where citrus in their huge trolley tubs
Were wheeled behind the glass walls
And spared each winter
Fresh lime grapefruit and orange
That's what a queen wants
That's what the orangery says
Now April's skies grow a little
More forgiving
Breaking into these tall columns
Of white clouds
                the kinds of elaborate
Shapes that children call God's Swans
Here in the country an hour
South of London
              where Gibbon finished

Decline and Fall in Lord Sheffield's library
In the manor house I can see just there
In the trees
                    as I walk with my friend along
The road that passes by his cottage
At the edge of the grounds of Sheffield Park
Once again
                    the sky's high pillars collect
Into one flat unrelieved blanket
Above these shivering leaves
And bent blades
                    a curtaining mist
Materializes out of the air
As we stop for a moment
On a stone bridge over the small falls
Between two of the lakes
And from the center of one of the lakes
A single swan glides toward us
Its wake a perfect spreading V
Widening along the water
                    as each arm
Of the V begins to break against
The lake's shores
                    the swan holds its head
And neck in a classical question mark
The crook of an old man's
Walking stick its eyes fixed on us
As it spreads its wings
In this exact feathery symmetry
Though it does not fly
                    simply lifting
Its head until the orange beak
Almost touches the apex of the stone
Arch of the bridge

Waiting for whatever crumbs we might
Have thought to bring
For a swan
        that now turns from us
Gliding with those same effortless gestures
Away without a glance back over
Its smooth shoulder
        the mist
Thickens as the clouds drop lower
And the rain threading the branches and leaves
Grows darker and more dense
Until I can barely see the swan on the water
Moving slowly as smoke through this haze
Covering the surface of the lake
That white smudge sailing
To whatever shelter it can find and as
I look again there's nothing
        only
The rain pocking the empty table
Of the lake
        so even the swan knows
Better than I to get out of the rain
The way it curled white as breath and rose
To nothing along the wind
        tonight
By the wood stove of the cottage
Drinking and talking with my friend
I'll tell him about the two women
I saw last week in Chelsea
One of them wrapped in a jumpsuit of wet
Black plastic
        her hair coal
Black greased and twirled into spikes
That fell like fingers onto her shoulders

But more alarming
                    those lines she'd drawn
Out from her mouth with an eyebrow pencil
Along her pale cheeks the perfect
Curved whiskers of a cat
And the other one
                    her friend dressed
In white canvas painter's pants white leather
Boots and a cellophane blouse
                              who'd dyed
Her hair utterly white then teased it
So that it rose
Or fell in the breeze lightly and stiffly
As feathers who'd painted her mouth
The same hard rubbery orange as a swan's
And even to a person of no great humor
Or imagination they were
                          these two
In the silent path they cut in the air
Along King's Road in every way
Beautiful
          and for the rest
Of the day I was so shaken I made
Myself stop for a drink in Soho
A strip joint called *The Blade*
I'd stumbled into and judging from my
Welcome not a place for the delicate
But I stuck it out through enough Scotch
To make me drunk fearless
And screaming through the first show
When at its end the final stripper
Stepped from the small stage right onto the bar top
Everyone clearing away the glasses and bottles
From the polished copper in front of them

As she threw off everything strutting
Down the narrow bar except
A white boa G-string
Shivering against her thighs as she
Kicked her silver high heels to either side
Then lay down in front of me
Her bare back and shoulders pressed flat
To the copper as it steamed and smudged beneath
Her body's heat
                    the catcalls and hollers
Rising as she lifted each leg
Pointing her toes to the spotlights scattered
Across the ceiling
                    her legs held in a pale V
The silver sequins of her high heels
Glittering in the lights but
Then she stood abruptly
And stepped back onto the stage not
Waiting a moment before turning her back
To the hoarse cheers
                    disappearing
In the sheer misty gauze of the old curtains
And as the lights came up there was
Where she'd been
Just the trails and webs of cigarette smoke
Those long curlicues in a tattoo of light
Those ghosts and feathers of dust
Still drifting down onto the bare tables
The glistening bar
                    onto the empty veiled stage
Of wood warped gently as waves

Black Poppy (At the Temple)

Perhaps it's a question of what
The ruins will accept   a simple flower
Or a few casual hymns by the side
Of this narrow mountain road
Where the dusty cones of sunlight are falling
Through the afternoon air
& the marble ribs of the temple are starting to blur
As the tourists come back across the fields

He slid down off the dented hood of the car
To open the door for them & acknowledge
Their praise of the view

Yet as he glanced out of habit into the side mirror
The hammered whiteness of his own face
Startled him & on
The drive back down the steep cobbled road
To the hotel in the valley   he knew that it was

Time he left his closet not a room at the rear
Of the hotel filled it seemed
With nothing but dull paintings & moldering books
& maps no one unfolded
                          time to walk away
From all of the habits that owned him especially
The habit of dreams

& that evening as he drove back up the road
Toward the crest of stars above the temple

Those ruins where he could walk & pray
To nothing

He knew that in every one of those dreams
He'd always be a dead man   just a suicide of
Elegant but precise intent
Dressed in a white summer suit & wearing
On his lapel an exquisite & dramatic black poppy

A hand-stitched blossom of glazed silk
Black as the shadow of a real poppy   black as
That moist bud of opium

Pinned to no memory of a living man

Chapter Forever

I remember I was 9 or 10   so the year I guess
Was 1959   my aunt was showing me the city
Of Sausalito   & the houseboats
Where some of her friends had once lived

On a patch of grass by the sidewalk
A girl sat with her legs crossed   holding
In her left hand a perfectly blank tablet
The size of a transistor radio   & in her right
An unused pen   she was staring right out
Into the Pacific   & as we walked by
My aunt shrugged & said *Too bad   No inspiration*

We passed a coffee shop
& in its doorway a couple stood just talking
He was on the top step & she was looking up at him
From the step below   he rubbed his beard   & as
We passed he winked at us   *That's Lenny Bruce*
My aunt said quietly & though we kept on walking
After a block or so   I turned around to see

He was still joking with the woman
Palms upturned he was slowly drawing both arms up
Into a full cross   his head fell limply to one side
& the woman started laughing even harder   I remember
She was laughing so hard pretty soon she was almost
Bent over   almost crying   I think   crying

An Essay on Liberation

He stood naked at one of the two windows
She kept open in all weathers in her
Corner room at the back of the old building
As the sun rose   he watched a man
Dragging a handcart along the narrow alley below
& across the court a young boy was turning
His face from side to side in a freckled mirror
From the temples in the old section of the city
He could hear the first sequence
Of morning prayers   & to the west he could see
The dulled bronze domes of The Church of the Orthodox
Where at any moment the bells would begin to chime
& in the streets crisscrossing the city
From the old section to the sea
The tanks & personnel trucks began moving quietly
Into position in their orderly & routine way
& the bells began sounding from their tower
They were answered by the echoing concussion of mortars
As the daily shelling of the hills began
& she was slicing small pieces of bread the size of coins
To fry in goat butter & chives   she was naked
Kneeling on one of the worn rugs thrown at angles across
The scarred floor   she glanced up at him & smiled
Nodding for no reason in particular   & in spite of
The fact the one phrase he'd taught her perfectly
Began with the word for *free*   though it ended
With *nothing*

The Man
in the Yellow Gloves

"They were kept in a wooden trunk
In one corner of the attic
A trunk my grandfather had painted
With red and black enamels
In the manner of the Chinese cabinets
He loved and could not afford
And inside the trunk the small box
Lined with a violet velvet
Where he kept his gloves
                              a box
That I believe should have held
A strand of pearls or a set
Of bone-handled
Carving knives from Geneva
A box fluted with ivory
And engraved with my grandfather's
Initials each letter
Still faintly visible in its flourish
Of script across the tiny brass shield
Holding the latch
                    one night
My mother dragged it out to remind
Herself of a particular
Summer at the lake when her father
Dressed to the teeth for once
In his life arrived at
The lake shore for a cocktail party

At a neighbor's boat and stepped
Right off into the water
Trying to stretch the short distance
From the dock to the boat's deck
And though the water was extremely shallow
All anyone could see for a moment
Were his hands held barely
Up in the twilight up
Above the surface of the water
Not pleading for help not reaching for
A rope but simply keeping his gloves
Dry his gloves of lemon silk
Which he refused to let touch water
Or liquid of any kind but
He rose slowly in the foam
Walking up the muddy rocks kicking
And swearing
Making his way over to the lake's edge
His hands still held up as if
At gunpoint
To the applause of the whole
Party my mother said as she worked
The frozen clasp loose of its pin
And slid her fingernail along
The edges of the box
Where the mold held it
Until the thin lid peeled back
And inside
            the yellow silk
Lit against the violet lining
Each finger of each glove bent
Slightly in an undisturbed
Calm
The two thumbs folded

Precisely across the palms
As if to guard the long seams
Crossing each like a lifeline
And my mother held the two gloves
Up to the light to let us see
Their transparence
                    a glow
Like the wings of a flying fish
As it clears the sea's surface
Then she laid them in my own
Cupped hands
Each as faintly moist as a breath
And as she smoothed them again
Along the velvet of their box
I imagined how I might someday pull
Them on in elegant company
Though even then the gloves were as small
As my hands
And so the next summer with my family
Camping near that familiar lake
I decided one night to find the old dock
Long since replaced by a new marina
I took the kerosene lamp
And walked to the main road
Then along its low curving shoulders
Until I came to the pitted asphalt lane
That once led to the dock
I picked my way slowly through the rubble
Through the brush and overgrown branches
The small globe of light thrown
By the lamp falling
Ahead of me along the path
Until I could see the brief glitter
And glare of the lake

Where the stars had escaped their clouds
And stood reflected
                        and where the road
Once swung gently toward the pier
The rocks now fell off 20 feet
In a sudden shelf and at its bottom
The dark planking of the dock began
I held the lamp in both hands
Pressing my back against
The slick dirt-and-stone face of the shelf
I slid carefully down working the heels
Of my boots into the crags and juts
To slow myself in the clatter
Of twigs and gravel old
Paving rotted boards and bark
Until I stopped and caught my breath
Looking out over the old dock
The soft planks at my feet stretching
Past the water's edge
Held up still by a few fat pilings
And as I took the first
Of a few steps
                        the moldered boards
Sagged and snapped beneath me splinters
Shooting up as I tried to leap clear
As one ankle twisted in the broken planks
And I fell face down onto the mossy
Dock the lamp
I'd been holding the whole time
Smashing in my hands the kerosene
Washing over the boards and my fingers
Up past both wrists and blazing
In a sudden and brilliant gasp of flame
I held up my burning hands

Yanking my leg up through the shattered boards
Rolling then falling onto the rocks below
My hands still aflame each a flat
Candle boned with five wicks
And then I remember only
The hospital in the village
Then the hospital in the city where
I lay for weeks
My hands bandaged and rebandaged
Like heavy wooden spoons
And beneath the crisp daily
Gauze the skin of each hand was seared
And blistered each finger raw
The pores dilating as the burnt skin
Was first bared to the air then to
The ointments
And each day more morphine
As the fever rose up my arms into
My mind my dreams until the morphine
Dimmed the nights and days
Until at last even I could stand to look
At the gnarled and shrunken hands
As if some child had made
The skeletons of wire
Then wrapped each poorly in doughy strings
of papier-mâché
                    in the next year
My hands were stitched in a patchwork
Of dime-sized pieces of skin cut
And lifted from the small
Of my back or my legs
Until they began to resemble
Hands you might hold in your own
But since then and in the hottest

Weather it doesn't matter I've
Always worn these gloves
Not from any
Vanity but to spare myself and you
The casual looking away
These gloves of kid leather tanned
Soft as skin and dyed at my request
A pale yellow
        the yellow of a winter lemon
In honor of my grandfather in honor
Of the fire as it dies
And if some men choose to walk
Miles in the country just
To look across the patches and divides
Of the landscape
Into the hills lakes and valleys
Or the dense levels of tree and cloud
So that they might better meditate upon
Their world their bitterness fatigue
Themselves well
I have only to take off one glove
Or another to stare down into the landscape
Of each scorched stitched hand
At the melted webs of flesh at the base
Of each finger
        the depressions
Or small mounts and lumps of scar
The barely covered bone
           or the palms
Burnt clean of any future any
Mystery so I'll pull back on
My gloves these
That I order each year from London
And if in the course of a dinner somewhere

I hear comments about the arrogance
Of a man who'd wear his gloves
Through an entire meal what a dandy
What an out-of-date mannered sort of parody
Of a gentleman
                    I will not mind
If the mild shock and disapproval rise
When I wear my yellow gloves
I'll never pull one off to startle
Or shame everyone into silence
                                instead
I'll simply check to see that each glove
Is properly secure
                    that each pearl button
Is snugly choked in its taut loop
Its minute noose of leather"

Leap of Faith

No less fabulous than the carved marble inner
Ear of a lost Michelangelo & more
Blinding than the multiple courts & interior facets
Of a black diamond held up in broken moonlight

This final geography acknowledges its trunks of
Ebony & its boughs of summer rain

Though there at the gate where Dante burned his
Initials into the face of the oak shield
I hesitated before following the switchback trail up
To the precipice overlooking the canyon the abyss
So relished by philosophy & when I saw you
On the opposite cliff in your long cape & gold
Shoes with frayed thin ribbons snaking up your ankles

Like anyone approaching from the foot of a bridge
I simply stepped toward you & below the bones
Of the fallen shone in the lightning & the prayers

& certainly it was there in that country
Braced between twin brackets of stone I saw only one
Belief remains for a man whose life is spared by

A faith more insupportable than air

No Heaven

This is the last prayer in the book
Of black prayers   a last
Passionate *yes*

Against bad timing & bad luck

& what else
Could be delivered beyond request
Except: *the living & the dead*

So I'll lay these carved shadow-figures

To rest along the rough rack pallet
Beneath the bed   though
Their shadows still continue   poor pilgrims

Walking the curved white stucco arch
Above our heads   & after
You wake to the scraping of these pine limbs
Against the unlatched windowpane

I'll smooth the delicate line & lace of sweat
That trims your hair's damp open fan
Along the folded pillow

The fever's watermark as it slowly stains
The forehead just as the tides of the canal

Measure these erratic summer rains
Streaking the sheer cement banks & high walls
As the debris of the city

Rises endlessly   & then endlessly falls

& I remember how the light with its simplicity
Frames always the lasting shape
Of your body   (standing)   at the jetty's end

& in the dream: *I'm running toward*

You to drape a silver raincoat   across your
Uncovered shoulders as you turn & the
World flares   & we wait

For an ending that grows irrevocably older
As in every apocalyptic play
& settling on us   upon the jetty   an ash colder

Than   in winter   the iron lattice
Of the cage I grip with both hands as I speak
To the albino mandrill   (at the Historical Zoo)

Not all but some days about the eclipse

Of earth   & flesh   & brick
Though no matter how I've tried   no matter
All of the horrible things I've said

The only response I can ever provoke

Is a few bared teeth as he throws
Back his head   & screams
                              Is that really
For all of the dead   a child by me
Asked her mother once & then she
Continued   *I mean all of the dead he remembers*

From his monkey dreams

In my dreams the world dies also in white embers

Not ash of course but blown light   drifting
Over the jetty   silently   forever

Yet this morning as I look very
Closely into the dresser mirror I can see
There in my own face

The hard meridian crossed & then re-crossed
    Hope   the new year

& yours is the name I'll say again & again

Until I'm sure this world can't force apart
The simple pulse of heaven
From the elaborate music of the heart

& all I want is for this sickness to have passed

Leaving us the ordinary world
Whole & rising in the dark   *this* world   *this* earth

& walking calmly toward us out of the broken mists

The figure whose passion remains the single
Gift   (yet) who now at last   admits
That we're to be given no heaven

No heaven   but this

IV. From *Terraces of Rain:*
An Italian Sketchbook

Ed io riverso
nel potere che grava attorno, cedo
al sortilegio di non riconoscere
di me più nulla fuor di me . . .

—Eugenio Montale

. . . Ma io, con il cuore cosciente
di chi soltanto nella storia ha vita,
potrò mai più con pura passione operare,
se so che la nostra storia è finita?

—Pier Paolo Pasolini
(1922-1975)

Terraces of Rain

And the mole crept along the garden,
And moonlight stroked the young buds of
The lemon trees, and they walked the five lands . . .
Sheer terraces, rocks rising
Straight up from the sea; the strung vines
Of the grapes, the upraised hands of the olives,
Presided and blessed. Between Vernazza
And Monterosso, along a path
Cut into the sea cliff, a place for lovers
To look down and consider their love,
They climbed up to the double-backed lane
Where a few old women gathered herbs
By the roadside. Voices —
Scattered in the hills above —
Fell like rushes in a wind, their rasp and echo
Traveling down and forever in the clear sea air . . .
Then clouds, then mist, then a universal gray . . .
Where Signore and Signora Bianchini are having lunch,
She stops to talk with them, weather being
The unavoidable topic. Slips of rain, a child's
Scrawl, sudden layers and pages — then, at last,
The fan of sunlight scraping clean
The sky. Here, the world's
Very old, very stubborn, and proud. In the twilight:
Shadow and other, watching the painted foam of
Waves running from the sunset
To the coves, the overturned skiffs, the white nets
Drying in the reddening air. She stood
Behind him, resting her hand on his shoulder. Night

Spread above them like a circling breeze,
The way a simple memory had once
Returned to Montale, calming his childhood
And a troubled winter sea. The air still cleansing,
She said, the heart that was uncleansable. The unforgiving
One, that heart. . . . A boy in an emerald sweater
Passed, out walking a mongrel in good spirits. Across
The scallop of bay, the boats began
Returning to the harbor. Silent. Harsh. Such country
Breaks the selfish heart. There is no original sin:
To be in love is to be granted the only grace
Of all women and all men.

(The Cinque Terre)

Francesco and Clare

It was there, in that little town
On top of the mountain, they walked,
Francesco and Chiara,
That's who they were, that's what
They told themselves — a joke, their joke
About two saints, failed lovers held apart
From the world of flesh, Francis and Clare,
Out walking the old city, two saints,
Sainted ones, holy, held close to the life . . .
Poverty, the pure life, the one
Life for Franziskus and Klara,
Stalwarts given
To the joys of God in heaven
And on earth, Mother, praising Brother Sun
And Sister Moon; twin saints, unified
In their beauty as one, Francisco and Clara,
A beauty said of God's will and word, bestowed
And polished by poverty, François
With Claire, the chosen poverty, the true
Poverty that would not be their lives . . .
And they took their favorite names, Clare and Francesco,
Walking the streets of stone the true saints
Walked, watching as the larks swirled
Above the serene towers, the larks
Francesco once described as the color
Of goodness, that is, of the earth, of the dead . . .
Larks who'd not seek for themselves any extravagant
Plumage, humble and simple, God's birds
Twirling and twisting up the pillowing air . . .

And Francesco said to Clare, *Oh little plant I love,*
My eyes are almost blind with Brother Sun . . . tell me,
Who hides inside God's time . . . ?
And Clare, rock of all Poor Clares, stood
In the warm piazza overlooking the valley, weary,
Her shoulder bag sagging from the weight
Of her maps and books, and said across the rain-slick
Asphalt of the parking lot, to the poor bird climbing
The wheel of sky it always had loved best,
Dear lark, dear saint, all my kisses on your nest!

(Assisi)

The Doors

The doors were oak, massive . . .
Their panels, bronze. The 12th century, a good
Century for fear, he thought, standing there
Before them, these doors of the oldest stories,
Parts of which had always been his life,
His many ancient lives —
It was a beautiful garden; he'd been sorry
To leave. When the boys, his sons, quarreled
And the one fell to the other, he searched
The sky, but the sky blew resolute and bronze . . .
Yet what he recalled most of the day
They left, he and she, were the outspread wings
Of the angel, each inscribed with heavy veins
Like the fronds of an enormous feathery
Palm, the plumage of a showgirl,
And the angel's breath, pungent as anise, fine
As the light rising off a mountain lake
In early autumn — *He thought*
Of the squat boat he must sail, the dove
Set loose above the storming waters,
Of the altar on the hillside and his young
Lamb of a son, of the bitter bronze speaking
At last, saying WAIT! . . . how he'd wept,
Waiting as he had always waited, before
These doors, silence . . .
And the doors repeated their stories: good, evil,
All the shavings of testament, or testimony —
Then, in the shifting dark, he saw her
Beginning the dance; though he

Felt his fear cocooned by her beauty as
The veils slowly fell, still, his shoulders ached
With the knowledge of the air ripped
By the falling sword. Her body was smeared
With oils and scents, covered with nothing except
The long silk loincloth
Wrapped haphazardly around her hips. She danced
Naming for the whole of the King's court
Every temptation worth dying for . . . as
She unwound the silk from her waist, draping
It loosely around his neck, passing
Slowly before every eye, before
Turning to claim her price. Of course, he knew
He should keep his head about this sort of thing,
But as the sweat ran down into his eyes,
He didn't. *O Sainted Zeno, doors of frozen decay*
Polished by pimps and pilgrims with the froth
Of their prayers, O . . . This was
What he tried to say, but his tongue grew
So swollen and thick. And his head felt so light,
Yet weary, like a baby's, cradled that way
In her delicate white arms.

(Verona; the Church of San Zeno)

Last Night with Rafaella

Last night, with Rafaella,

I sat at one of the outside tables
At *Rosati* watching the *ragazzi* on Vespas
Scream through the Piazza del Popolo

And talked again about changing my life,

Doing something meaningful — perhaps
Exploring a continent or discovering a vaccine,
Falling in love or over the white falls
Of a dramatic South American river! —
And Rafaella

Stroked the back of my wrist as I talked,

Smoothing the hairs until they lay as quietly
As wheat before the old authoritarian wind.

Rafaella had just returned from Milano
Where she'd supervised the Spring collection
Of a famous, even notorious, young designer —

A man whose name brought tears to the eyes
Of contessas, movie stars, and diplomats' wives
Along the Via Condotti or the Rue
Du Faubourg-St-Honoré.

So I felt comfortable there, with Rafaella,
Discussing these many important things, I mean

The spiritual life, and my own
Long disenchantment with the ordinary world.

Comfortable because I knew she was a sophisticated,
Well-traveled woman, so impossible
To shock. A friend who'd
Often rub the opal on her finger so slowly

It made your mouth water,

The whole while telling you what it would be like
To feel her tongue addressing your ear.

And how could I not trust the advice
Of a woman who, with the ball of her exquisite thumb,
Carefully flared rouge along the white cheekbones
Of the most beautiful women in the world?

Last night, as we lay in the dark,
The windows of her bedroom open to the cypress,
To the stars, to the wind knocking at those stiff
Umbrella pines along her garden's edge,
I noticed as she turned slowly in the moonlight

A small tattoo just above her hip bone —

It was a dove in flight or an angel with its
Head tucked beneath its wing,

I couldn't tell in the shadows . . .

And as I kissed this new illumination of her body
Rafaella said, *Do you know how to tell a model?*
In fashion, they wear tattoos like singular beads
Along their hips,
                    but artists' models

Wear them like badges against the daily nakedness,
The way Celestine has above one nipple that
Minute yellow bee and above
The other an elaborate, cupped poppy . . .

I thought about this,
Pouring myself a little wine and listening
To the owls marking the distances, the geometries
Of the dark.
                Rafaella's skin was
Slightly damp as I ran my fingertip
Along each delicate winged ridge of her
Collarbone, running the harp length of ribs
Before circling the shy angel . . .

And slowly, as the stars
Shifted in their rack of black complexities above,

Along my shoulder, Rafaella's hair fell in coils,

Like the frayed silk of some ancient tapestry,
Like the spun cocoons of the Orient —
Like a fragile ladder

To some whole other level of the breath.

(Rome)

To Pasolini

I. At Italo's

Out in the visible city, the heart
Of the night spreads its soft
Black petals. Slowly, the *ragazzi* start

Moving along the streets. A few drift off
Into the piazza below, trading
Cigarettes, phone numbers, jokes. The exhaust

Of Roman traffic thins . . . and finally fades.
The girls, shaking their heads of loose curls;
The boys, exhaling like they've got it made.

Up in Italo's apartment, planets of ice swirl
In my glass, opaque and tinted gold
By the scotch. The room is the color of pearl.

Pier Paolo, Italo tells about the butcher's kid
You picked up the night you died, the bruise
Left along the sallow, broad

Curve of your cheek. Italo says you cruised
Every night of your life — that test
A man makes in the dark. Does any man get used

To the test? If so, not to the scent of death
Hardening in the air like Roman dust,
Stealing its rhythm from every broken breath,

Leaving a shirt flaked with rust,
No, blood and bits of . . . we know the rest;
We know almost as much as we must —

We know most things hurt; we know this best.
Italo turns to me and says, "Every night of
His life . . . he spent out in the wilderness."

II. Ostia

The orphans of the heart must turn to thee
Byron said of Rome, though he could have meant
The way they turned to you, as easily.

The boys standing outside the station have spent
Their last *lire*. Looking for more, looking tough,
One joins you to Ostia, where you often went.

The seaplane basin fills quietly with shadow.
Your immaculate gray Alfa sits a few
Moments, hood still warm, motor switched off . . .

Starlight litters the slowly falling dew;
A man falls to his hands and shattered knees.
The sky streaks with violet veins, then blue.

Mama. Mama. They are killing me . . .

III. 1984

Last night at dinner at *Vecchia Roma*,
Downing *fettucine ai carciofi*
With my favorite bottle of Boggio,

A young woman I didn't know turned to me —
She was a friend of the friend whose birthday
We'd been celebrating, her hand on my knee

Like an old lover's — and what could I say
When she asked about you, whom I'd never known?
Yet something took me over, the way

In a dream one suddenly feels at home
In even the oddest circumstances. I talked
Endlessly, just the two of us alone,

About those last few days before your death,
Your murder . . . This morning, at my study —
Hung over, depressed — I tried to clear my head

With cup after cup of black, muddied
Espresso. I went out and stood with my back
To the old Aurelian wall, the funny

Garden stretched out below me. The arced black
Limbs of the umbrella pines, all lined
With sparrows; lizards, dancing along the stacks

Of the white bricks. I watched that first fine
Resurrection of the mist just rising
In the early haze of the morning sunlight . . .

Then it hit me, like a simple fist clenched
Against the fact, against the earth —
Last night had been November the second,

The ninth anniversary of your death.

IV. Una Vita Violenta (1955)

Many children in only one bed,
An outdoor toilet, a typical Roman slum
Where half of the sons end up in jail or dead

By the time they're fifteen. To get ahead
In this life you can't be as dumb
As the other boys beside you in the bed,

The brothers who cry simply to be fed,
Who cry until adolescence comes,
Then end up in jail or dead.

Some get lucky. In the park, given head
By some prosperous client, they roll him,
Or become one of the few in his bed,

Living longer this way, staying fed
And clothed, even having a little fun
Before going to jail or ending up dead.

They're all my boys, Pier Paolo said,
From the streets and gutters and the slums;
So many to save from the Tiber's cold bed —

Then God divides: These to jail, these dead.

V. *The Art of Argument, The Argument of Art*

Before our lunch, lovely G tries to explain
How it works with Roman artists of *any*
Kind — writers, sculptors, directors — "Pains

In the ass, all of them; but I swear not many
Were as stubborn as Pier Paolo. Once,
He and T" (her husband) "argued three days running;

First one, then the other, taking his stance
About *'Theater'* — for T, it was art;
For Pier Paolo, art didn't stand a chance.

He said theater should play its part
As a political tool, 'a necessary vehicle
To educate and liberate.' So they'd both start

Shouting at each other, ridiculing
The other's position; only, when it got very late,
Pier Paolo'd go home to sleep — he was no fool —

But! He'd be back early! He couldn't *wait*
To begin the argument again. Still, after
Three days, they both quit. Pasolini walked straight

Out the door and never, I mean not once *ever*
Did he and T speak. It was just nuts;
Two close friends so furious with each other

They go the rest of their lives without
Talking — *or* arguing — for all those years. Dull?
No; but Roman grudges! What a way to live out

One's life, eh? Paranoid, bitter, just enough
Fame to be smug, which is already too much.
It's true not all of us have it so rough;

Besides, an artist's life is always such
Pleasant torture here in Rome, who'd want
To be elsewhere? Now, how about some lunch?"

First, I pour us more wine to drink.
She sighs, then shrugs: "You see,
We argue about really everything we think —

I think it's how we learn what we believe."

VI. Winter Sun

It's mid–December in Rome, yet the sun's
Been blazing all week. The air's brisk,
Chilly, then very cold at night when,

If the sky is clear, the clouds all whisked
Away, the searing constellations beat down.
Some mornings, leaves flare and burn like old lists

Out by the gardener's shed. Along the lawn,
The paths marked by low shrubs rustle and whine
With lizards as I pass. Azaleas, newly blown,

Rock in the flower beds. The quiet pines,
Stately and aloof, fill yet again with sparrows.
Each afternoon, I pour a glass of wine

And watch those sparrows fall and swoop above
Some morsel of worm or bug. From the cracks
In the Aurelian wall, the lizards come

Crawling onto the bleached bricks, to bask
In the steady sun. They have nothing to fear;
At least, nothing but the quick shadow cast

As I lean back in my chair. It's quiet here,
Away from the farting Vespas and the acrid
City air. I look over the garden, where

The smoke of the burning leaves still drifts
Above the heads of the wildflowers. *To
Live is to struggle, to struggle is to live* —

That's what you said. Pier Paolo, whose
                    Love are we so terrified to lose?

VII. Hotel of Ash

The hotel room is tawdry, nondescript;
There is a narrow cot, a straight-backed chair,
A dresser with a huge mirror that barely fits

Between the single window and the closet door.
The boy pulls the chair right up to the dresser,
Reaching out to tilt the beveled mirror

Until he sits before his image, there —
Reflected. He waits. The room reeks and sways.
He flips his cigarette butt into the air,

Toward the old tin of ashes, and says
To no one, "*Bless me, Father . . .*" He picks up
The worn muslin curtain, where it lies

Crumpled on the floor; he spreads it out.
He scatters the ashes from the cigarette tin
And rubs them slowly over the whole cloth

Until the muslin has been blackened
Like a mourning veil. Over the low, angled
Image of himself he drapes the ashen curtain,

And sits back again in the mangled,
Rickety chair. Its wood, completely scarred
By knifed initials, burns. His face, an angel's

Reflected in the quiet of the mirror,
Though now only faintly visible
Behind the dark muslin, the hung, tarred

Veil of his homemade confessional.
Behind its curtain, in the silver glass,
The Angel of Forgiveness is reasonable,

And waiting. Waiting for this silence
To be broken, for the boy at the dresser
To begin his story of concluding violence.

He shrugs and, as if still without a care,
Lights another cigarette. The breeze
From the window mutters in the ashen air;

Angel-breath, mirror fog: the man's pleas
As the board smashes against his head —
The Alfa no longer purring like the sea . . .

The boy continues until Pasolini's nearly dead,
Then gets into the lean gray car
And backs over him, then forward, across his head.

Now the boy lifts his eyes to this horror
Of himself: the mask of the dead angel
Hanging before him in the blowing mirror . . .

The face of Pasolini pulsing on the skull
Where the boy's own face should be —
Confessor, and victim. The rippling veil

Torn between the two worlds. The sea
Slapping the coast of Ostia, the seaplane
Basin quiet now. The murmuring gray

Alfa, the boy at the wheel, turns toward dawn,
Toward Rome . . . the corpse jerks once or twice.
And Pasolini's ghost smirks: "*Cut. Cut. FIN!*"

Here, the scene suffers its awkward splice —
The boy's head falls forward onto his chest.
Days roll slowly in the sky, black dice . . .

Pasolini said he'd never die like the rest;
I'm not sure *this* is what he meant.
Though, possibly . . . the ash, its blunt kiss

Still printed on his cheek . . . the wood, bent.
What better place to die than near the sea?
Which coins still left to spill? Which spent?

VIII. Love for the Dragon

History is blood; or so history says.
There are some lessons we'd rather not learn.
For Pasolini, the question was, each day:

How does one live? What can one *do*, I mean.
He believed beliefs should be fiercely held,
This most public of private men —

One must: 1) Love poetry after poetry's death;
2) Remain *of* the spirit without a God;
3) Trust always in the beauty of the raw;

4) Meld the contemplative with the active world;
5) Piss stylishly in the face of repression;
6) Simply refuse to be bored;

7) Wildly annihilate one's own reputation;
8) Go out every night
Religiously, taking the body's dictation;

9) Regard history as the soul's spotlight,
And fix one's place in its theater;
10) Never forget what it meant to be truly poor.

Who could think of anything better?
Except perhaps to remain,
As Pasolini wished to, the child of this letter:

Dear _____: Sitting by the small stone fountain
At the Villa Sciarra, with a little time to spend;
The white wisteria's slowly blooming again

On the laced arbor above — winter's end,
At last. A boy in green khaki shorts just passed,
Followed by his mother and her "friend,"

A man too suave, too slick, too crass
To be the boy's father. Besides, the boy
Paid no attention to him at all, this last

Of his mother's men. The boy dragged an old toy
Dragon behind him on a short gold cord,
Its mouth spitting little friction sparks of joy —

He circled the fountain like a tiny Chinese lord,
Secure in his wild love for the dragon,
Its steady metallic pulse all that any of us heard.

His mother called out to him, as did her "friend";
Yet they, like the world, were triumphantly ignored.
Ah, I thought, to be *that* powerful! To have again,

As a boy, a dragon on a leash! And to be heard
In one's own pure defiant silence —
To have again a dragon's voice; I mean, that is . . .

the last word.

v. *Merlin:*
New Poems

*Toute chose sacrée et qui veut demeurer
sacrée s'enveloppe de mystère.*

—Mallarmé

I Know

The definition of beauty is easy;
it is what leads to desperation.
—Valéry

I know the moon is troubling;

Its pale eloquence is always such a meddling,
Intrusive lie. I know the pearl sheen of the sheets
Remains the screen I'll draw back against the night;

I know all of those silences invented for me approximate
Those real silences I cannot lose to daylight . . .
I know the orchid smell of your skin

The way I know the blackened path to the marina,
When gathering clouds obscure the summer moon —
Just as I know the chambered heart where I begin.

I know too the lacquered jewel box, its obsidian patina;
The sexual trumpeting of the diving, sweeping loons . . .
I know the slow combinations of the night, & the glow

Of fireflies, deepening the shadows of all I do not know.

107

My Friend

My friend, a man I love as wholly,
      As deeply as the brother neither of us
          Ever had, my friend, who once
Greeted me at the door of his carriage house —
          Having not seen each other in seven years —
      Saying only, as he turned to place
The needle into the grooves of Mahler's unfinished 10th,
      "*Listen* to this! It's just like the *Four Quartets*!"
          His head, tilted slightly back
As we listened in silence, his black scarf looped loosely
      Around his neck, not an affectation, simply
Because of the cold in the carriage house he'd redone
          With everything but heat,
      The wind slicing off the East River, the mansion
In front of us lit up brilliantly that night
          By chandelier and firelight — my friend,
      Whom I love as deeply as any friend, called
This morning to report the sleet blanketing the East,
          To ask about the color of the sunlight
Sweeping the beaches of California; I tell him, "A lot
          Like the green of ice at night,
      Or the orange of the hair of that girl who once
Lived downstairs from you, in Cleveland. . . ."
          My friend, who said nothing for a moment,
      My friend, who had always lived the pure, whole
Solitude of Rilke, though he fell in love
          As often and as desperately as Rilke,
      Began to talk about his recent engagement, now
Past, though still not quite a memory, simply a subject

Yet too mystifying to be ignored,
To a debutante, half-British, that is, an American deb
With an overlay of aristocratic parquet —
Albeit with an Italian given name — a stunning woman
He had loved desperately, silently,
The way Rilke loved
The sky at evening as the cloud-laced sunset
Dusted the high ragged peaks of Switzerland . . .
Yet, after a pause, he began
Again to talk, about some new acquaintances, two
Young ladies, both painters (of course),
Who seemed to enjoy his company as a pair; that is,
The two of them, both of the young
Ladies, preferred him as a garnish
To their own extravagances — for example,
They'd welcomed him into their bath one
Evening when he came to visit, only to find them lathering
Each other tenderly. And though quite
Clearly desiring the company of each other to his alone,
They were tolerant, he said, even welcoming,
As the one reached up her hand
And invited him into the froth of the square black tub.
And now this had, he reported, been
Going on for several weeks this way, perhaps longer,
He couldn't be clear about those kinds
Of details, though about other, more
Intriguing things, his memory was exact. The very night before,
He recalled, as the two young women painted
His naked torso slowly into a tuxedo of pastel
Watercolors, they'd both wisely proposed the following:
A joint — triadic — marriage for one month
As they traveled, all three, through Italy and France,
A journey to visit all of the Holy Places
Of Art, as well as
The grandparents of the one, Delphine — about whom Constance,

The younger, had heard so many stories — at their home
In the hills overlooking the beaches of Nice.
My friend, a quiet man, a man who remains as
Precise, in his reckonings, as a jewel cutter, a man whose
Charm could seduce the Medusa, was,
He confessed, totally at a loss, bewildered, delighted,
Terrified, exhausted — mainly, he said, exhausted
From the constellations of couplings
He'd been exercising, recognizing in the process
He was, as they say, as he said, really not quite so young
As he'd once been, though certainly still
As eager for invention
As any artist who takes his life work, well, seriously . . .
And as we talked about old times, old friends, our
Old lives being somehow perpetually rearranged, at last
He stopped me, saying, "Christ, you know —
I can't *believe* how much the world has changed. . . ."

My Tea with Madame Descartes

She'd said let's have tea
Because she believed I was English; she meant,
            Of course, not tea but her usual sequence
Of afternoon aperitifs, in slender glasses the length
            Of a finger, and only slightly wider.
                  We met near the Odéon because, she said,
For her, all the cafés in Montparnasse were haunted still;
            Just like, she added, the old days with S——.
I'd spent the morning looking through the file drawers
            Of the *Herald Tribune*, leafing through early reviews
                  Of Madame's stage days, then dozens of articles
About her books of photographs, her memoirs, the late novel
            That embarrassed several continents. Here and there,
I'd run across a few glossy photos of Madame herself
            Thrown into the file, always with yet
Another notable lovestruck admirer at her slender, bare elbow.
            When I walked in, still a little blinded by
The September sunlight, I didn't notice her at first, tucked
            Along the far wall, a leisurely veil
Of cigarette smoke steadily latticing the air before her;
            Then I caught her unmistakable reflection
In one of the square mirrored pillars, those regal cheekbones,
            The nearly opaque, sea-blue eyes
That'd commandeered both men and newspapers for forty years,
                        Simply lifting to meet mine . . .
As I introduced myself, my apologies for my late arrival
            Waved away like so much smoke,

I noticed that the silver of her hair was laced
With an astonishing gold, like those threads woven so deftly
              Throughout a tapestry to trap the light;
In that dim café, the gold fired as delicately as filaments
       Of beaten leaf in a Byzantine mosaic. Beneath her
                     Quite carefully constructed mask,
       The islands of rouge mapping soft slopes of powder,
Beneath the precise calm she'd expertly painted for herself
              Before the mirror, I could see
              Why scandal had tattooed even the air she'd
Walked through. I'd never seen a beauty like hers, riveting
                     As the Unicorn's
       Soft eye. There's so much we name as beautiful
Simply to dismiss it, cage it, desire then dispense with it —
              Yet her beauty was singular,
Volcanic, viscous . . . as inevitable as lava moving slowly
       Toward you. Even those few lines in her face
Seemed as delicate as those left by a leaf's edge, drawn by
              A child through the sand. Her beauty
       Was so close to a vengeance — one exacted by the world
Upon those of us so ordinary, so weak, we can barely
       Admit its existence. So I just sat there, a notebook
At hand; I took out my micro pocket recorder, placing it
                     Between us. She lit up a filtered Gitane;
Then she began: "I suppose I think the War years
                     Were the worst, always seeing some of one's
Old friends in swank restaurants lifting glasses
       To the Germans at adjoining tables, while the others
Had all disappeared into the Underground. At times, it was
                     So hard to know who still
       Might be alive. After the war, I took several lovers;
Then, the fatigue set in. I married a sweet but stupid man,
              A lawyer for Lanvin and Charvet; I slowly
Went mad, truly mad, living that way —

But getting out was almost accidental.
One fall, my friend Lee Miller happened to pass through Paris;
In the old days, I'd modeled nude for her crowd —
'Dusting off the lazy angels'
We called the parties we threw then. That visit, Lee
Gave me an old Rolliflex she'd outgrown,
And I thought, one day, flipping through those
Old pieces of hers from *Vogue* and *Life*, I'd like
To do that! About this time, my dull husband decided
We'd visit his brother, a sniffy diplomat off rotting
In Saigon. So, I packed my Rolliflex, knowing
That was that; when my husband went back to Paris,
I kissed him goodbye and took the train to Tibet — Lhasa —
Then on to Bangkok, Argentina, Chile . . .
Just everywhere. The whole while, I was learning
What the lens of my eye meant in the world.
I began to keep some journals too; slowly, I acquired
What's politely called *a kind of reputation*. Then,
I could get in anywhere — the refugee camps, prisons, anywhere!
Nobody would say *no* to me, the woman
With the famous eye, 'that daunting feminine aperture'
One pig of an editor called it. You know, the only photos
People remember are the most
Grotesque: the young African shepherd girl, hanging
By a loop of barbed wire; that charred carapace of a soldier's
Corpse, stretched out over the white coals
Of St. Lawrence's faithful grill . . .
Those heads of Buddhist monks nodding on a row of bamboo
  spikes.
Do you need more? I'm tired. Thank God that, in Saigon,
I threw caution right out along the winds;
For such an illogical woman
I suppose that's the last 'logical' thing I've ever done.
And now," she said, "put your notebook down; I've

Decided to take your picture."
Out of her purse, she pulled a spy-sized Minox, the kind
  With a drawbridge lens. As the tiny camera unfolded,
    The eye of its castle widening slowly
Before her consoling wink, I simply sat back, trying somehow
  To smile, to look worldly, desirable, nonchalant —
My hands so self-consciously gripping the small café table
    Which Madame had so easily turned.

Meditation

after Baudelaire

Quiet now, sorrow; relax. Calm down, fear . . .
You wanted the night? It's falling, here,
Like a black glove onto the city,
Giving a few some peace . . . but not me.

I think, well, almost everyone I know
Loves to be whipped by pleasure — right, Killer? —
As they stroll the boardwalk, parading their despair.
So why don't you come too? But instead, with me,

Away from all these tattered ghosts leaning off
The sky's balcony like last year's lovers;
We'll watch everything we regret step from the sea

Dripping . . . while the dead sun drags its arc
Towards China. Shroud of my heart, listen. Listen —
How softly the night steps toward us.

Lucifer in Starlight

Tired of his dark dominion . . .
—George Meredith

It was something I'd overheard
One evening at a party; a man I liked enormously
      Saying to a mutual friend, a woman
Wearing a vest embroidered with scarlet and violet tulips
      That belled below each breast, "Well, I've always
Preferred Athens; Greece seems to me a country
      Of the day — Rome, I'm afraid, strikes me
As being a city of the night . . . "
      Of course, I knew instantly just what he meant —
      Not simply because I love
Standing on the terrace of my apartment on a clear evening
      As the constellations pulse low in the Roman sky,
The whole mind of night that I know so well
      Shimmering in its elaborate webs of infinite,
Almost divine irony. No, and it wasn't only that Rome
      Was *my* city of the night, that it was here I'd chosen
      To live when I grew tired of my ancient life
As the Underground Man. And it wasn't that Rome's darkness
      Was of the kind that consoles so many
      Vacancies of the soul; my Rome, with its endless history
Of falls . . . No, it was that this dark was the deep, sensual dark
      Of the dreamer; this dark was like the violet fur
Spread to reveal the illuminated nipples of
      The She-Wolf — all the sequins above in sequence,
The white buds lost in those fields of ever-deepening gentians,

A dark like the polished back of a mirror,
            The pool of the night scalloped and hanging
Above me, the inverted reflection of a last,
                        Odd Narcissus . . .

                        One night my friend Nico came by
Close to three A.M. — As we drank a little wine, I could see
            The black of her pupils blown wide,
The spread ripples of the opiate night . . . And Nico
        Pulled herself close to me, her mouth almost
            Touching my mouth, as she sighed, "Look . . . ,"
And deep within the pupil of her left eye,
        Almost like the mirage of a ship's distant, hanging
            Lantern rocking with the waves,
I could see, at the most remote end of the receding,
        Circular hallway of her eye, there, at its doorway,
At the small aperture of the black telescope of the pupil,
                A tiny, dangling crucifix —
Silver, lit by the ragged shards of starlight, reflecting
        In her as quietly as pain, as simply as pain . . .
Some years later, I saw Nico on stage in New York, singing
        Inside loosed sheets of shattered light, a fluid
Kaleidoscope washing over her — the way any naked,
            Emerging Venus steps up along the scalloped lip
        Of her shell, innocent and raw as fate, slowly
Obscured by a florescence that reveals her simple, deadly
                Love of sexual sincerity . . .
        I didn't bother to say hello. I decided to remember
The way in Rome, out driving at night, she'd laugh as she let
        Her head fall back against the cracked, red leather
                Of my old Lancia's seats, the soft black wind
Fanning her pale, chalky hair out along its currents,
        Ivory waves of starlight breaking above us in the leaves;
The sad, lucent malevolence of the heavens, falling . . .
            Both of us racing silently as light. Nowhere,
Then forever . . .
                Into the mind of the Roman night.

A Fan Sketched
with Silver Egrets

hommage à Mallarmé

With no language
Except this single pulse, its shadow beating
Along the sky-domed ceiling of the room,
You sweep the open wing
Across your body with a singular gesture
Of pleasure, this messenger
Brushing the air so near my face — And so . . .
You need not speak. As this flight of egrets
Across the silk mask, this fan
Held so softly to your lips,
Seems to break apart as slowly
As blown ash, feathers rippling in the heavy
Weather of evening, you need not speak . . . even here,
Concealed by this soft wing (like a mirror
Trembling, like Narcissus's own breath),
As I lean closer to you, ready to step
Into a future so pure we will both lose
Our separate ways — come, now, out onto the terrace,
Let your breath freeze,
And rise, like frosted roses as they strike the night air,
The fan's gilled wing of light
Still guarded by your hand, like an egret diving
In its long free fall . . . this sense of the heavens
Opening as your kiss unfolds, this sense of you,
This scent of animal pleasure, an animal paradise
More savage than each corner of your mouth,
The subtle lie of your lips revealed by
These collapsing accordion pleats, the ripple of eyelash-

Painted silk . . . poor prisoners,
Those falling egrets folded in upon themselves in sleep
Stilled by the passage of
A summer moon along the fine tips of branches
Feathering the hillside. And so, you need not
Speak, later, as the last, soft
Silver skin of lace drops from your slender shoulders
Onto the floor, as you sit so silently
At your low, black lacquer vanity,
Its city of tiny glass towers, icy spires
Of perfume bottles, ancient flacons and phials —
Here, on the calm black surface of the vanity . . . here,
You'll place your wand, your folded sceptre,
This ivory baton meant to divine some future
Water, its future body, where every sleek egret slowly
Opens its wings like delicately blown sails
As it descends so simply onto the sheets of the waves,
Legs outstretched in flight,
The beating of each stroke bringing you closer
To the breathless surface of the pool
Where a boy leans close, then closer,
His face obscured at last by these falling bodies of light,
This mirror of his kiss broken as the whole
Of the night awaits
That moment his face becomes your own, my own, as
I stand behind you,
The severe white pleats of my evening shirt
Reflected in the vanity's glass,
Your eyes now black as the ebony studs along my breastbone —
And it's the way you pose,
The girl in Monsieur Manet's
Staged portrait, the familiar, stiff-spined
Fan, closing like an exhausted concertina,
Thin as a child's ruler, light
As a conductor's white orchestral commands . . .

This fan I've given you,
Sent from China by a friend, sketched with pale,
Thin cypress, and seven silver egrets; this fan, the one there,
Beneath your hand, beside that bracelet you love,
The gold one you wear like a barely manacled passion,
Your father's final gift —
Your fan remains . . . a closed half-moon of mask,
Alongside this pile of fire, those linked flames
Of the bracelet, that fragile pyre no longer burning
Except in the blackest evenings. Sometimes, as in all
The tapestries of breath, his breath,
That you recall, you can feel those echoes of silver wings,
Perhaps each of those moments
You look at me like a stranger in a stranger's mirror,
As the spread tail of the peacock in the garden
Rises to greet
The one last urgency of his life —
Then, even then, as you slowly lower the silk mask,
Your lips blushed by flame, flecked silver with feathered ash,
You will remember, as you must now, folded silently
Into my arms, you need not, of his death
Or any sorrow, speak . . .

120

Mercenary Muse

after Baudelaire

Well, heart's muse, lover, mistress of palaces,
When January cuts loose its northern winds, will you have
In the bitter, boring blackness of the snowy evenings
Even a few embers to warm your violet feet?

And how can you melt your icy, marble shoulders
With just those faint rays of starlight piercing the shutters?
Touch your purse — empty as your palace — and so, what now?
Will you harvest gold from the vaults of the sky?

Look, if you need to earn your nightly bread,
You should be like the playful choirboy swinging his censer,
Singing hymns you can scarcely believe . . .

Or, starved sexual acrobat, simply bare your breasts
And let your cool laughter, steeped in those tears nobody sees,
Blow away all of the vulgar spleen of the common man.

Los Angeles, 1954

It was in the old days,
When she used to hang out at a place
                    Called *Club Zombie*,
A black cabaret that the police liked
        To raid now and then. As she
                    Stepped through the door, the light
        Would hit her platinum hair,
And believe me, heads would turn. Maestro
                    Loved it; he'd have her by
The arm as he led us through the packed crowd
                    To a private corner
Where her secluded oak table always waited.
        She'd say, *Jordan* . . .
                            And I'd order her usual,
A champagne cocktail with a tall shot of bourbon
                    On the side. She'd let her eyes
        Trail the length of the sleek neck
                    Of the old stand-up bass, as
The bass player knocked out the bottom line,
                His forehead glowing, glossy
                            With sweat in the blue lights;
Her own face, smooth and shining, as
                The liquor slowly blanketed the pills
                            She'd slipped beneath her tongue.
Maestro'd kick the shit out of anybody
                Who tried to sneak up for an autograph;
He'd say, *Jordan, just let me know if*
                Somebody gets too close . . .
        Then he'd turn to her and whisper, *Here's*
Where you get to be Miss Nobody . . .

And she'd smile as she let him
Kiss her hand. For a while, there was a singer
At the club, a guy named Louis —
But Maestro'd changed his name to "Michael Champion";
Well, when this guy leaned forward,
Cradling the microphone in his huge hands,
All the legs went weak
Underneath the ladies.
He'd look over at her, letting his eyelids
Droop real low, singing, *Oh Baby I . . .*
Oh Baby I Love . . .   I Love You . . .
And she'd be gone, those little mermaid tears
Running down her cheeks. Maestro
Was always cool. He'd let them use his room upstairs,
Sometimes, because they couldn't go out —
Black and white couldn't mix like that then.
I mean, think about it —
This kid star and a cool beauty who made King Cole
Sound raw? No, they had to keep it
To the club; though sometimes,
Near the end, he'd come out to her place
At the beach, always taking the iced whiskey
I brought to him with a sly, sweet smile.
Once, sweeping his arm out in a slow
Half-circle, the way at the club he'd
Show the audience how far his endless love
Had grown, he marked
The circumference of the glare whitening the patio
Where her friends all sat, sunglasses
Masking their eyes . . .
And he said to me, *Jordan, why do*
White people love the sun so? —
God's spotlight, my man?
Leaning back, he looked over to where she

Stood at one end of the patio, watching
The breakers flatten along the beach below,
Her body reflected and mirrored
Perfectly in the bedroom's sliding black glass
Door. He stared at her
Reflection for a while, then looked up at me
And said, *Jordan, I think that I must be*
Like a pool of water in a cave that sometimes
She steps into . . .
Later, as I drove him back into the city,
He hummed a Bessie Smith tune he'd sing
For her, but he didn't say a word until
We stopped at last back at the club. He stepped
Slowly out of the back
Of the Cadillac, and reaching to shake my hand
Through the open driver's window, said,
My man, Jordan . . .   Goodbye.

"Who Is She . . ."

after Cavalcanti

Who is she, coming along the street, turning the heads
    Of men and angels, making the night air so
Tense, so trembling with clarity that even those poets
    Who adore ranting about love can only sigh?

And God! When she just happens to glance your way, well,
    Let love tell it, I can't even begin
To describe the way her modesty makes other women
    Grovel and weep in utter wretchedness.

And nothing I can say is really relevant; every word simply
    Grows transparent held up to her body, draped
In a cloak woven by time, threads of beauty and Godhead . . .

No surprise that our lofty ideals and tender, healing voices
    All fade before such an extravagance of grace —
Whose charms we'll never hold, in our minds, nor in our arms.

Merlin

Italo Calvino (1923–1985)

It was like a cave of snow, no . . .
More like that temple of frosted, milk-veined marble
       I came upon one evening in Selinunte,
Athena's white owl flying suddenly out of its open eaves.
     I saw the walls lined with slender black-spined
        Texts, rolled codices, heavy leather-bound volumes
Of the mysteries. Ancient masks of beaten copper and tin,
     All ornamented with rare feathers, scattered jewels.
His table was filled with meditative beakers, bubbling
        Here and there like clocks; the soldierly
Rows of slim vials were labeled in several foreign hands.
     Stacks of parchments, cosmological recipes, nature's
Wild equivalencies. A globe's golden armature of the earth,
        Its movable bones ringing a core of empty
     Space. High above the chair, a hanging Oriental scroll,
Like the origami of a crane unfolded, the Universe inked
        So blue it seemed almost ebony in daylight,
The stars and their courses plotted along its shallow folds
     In a luminous silver paint. On an ivory pole,
        His chameleon robe, draped casually, hieroglyphics
Passing over it as across a movie screen, odd formulas
     Projected endlessly — its elaborate layers of
Embroidery depicting impossible mathematical equations;
        Stitched along the hem, the lyrics
Of every song one hears the nightingale sing, as dusk falls
     On summer evenings. All of our stories so much

Of the world they must be spoken by
A voice that rests beyond it . . . his voice, its ideal melody,
Its fragile elegance guiding our paper boats,
Our so slowly burning wings,
Towards any immanent imagination, our horizon's carved sunset,
The last wisdoms of Avalon.

VI. *Coda*

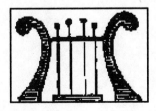

Study for the World's Body

THE BODY OF DESIRE

*

The self is empty, as empty
As a word. This is a simple truth
We all deny we know. Yet
The life of the body is waiting,
Waiting always, to be heard;
The one body of the still
Unwritten world. We redraw
Those woven borders of the soul,
Map again some faithful, raw
Region of the spirit, &
Pulling ourselves yet closer
To every breath of the *other*,
We give one final glance over
The shoulder, to see if what
One loves is still following,
Or lost; if that singular
Body of desire
Is still present, or remains.
The grace, the grave, & weight
Of the body still holding us
To earth. The shapes, the shell,
& shallow stare of the body
Suffering its flesh, its illness–
Carved hollows, its bare afflictions . . .
Those hopes we were the remnants of,

Of Time & the Body

(To HM, 1922–1987)

Is there a story? Where
Are the voices
Like the murmur of
The audience just before
The curtain rises? Is
There another way
To begin, now, without
The film blistering
In the glare,
Each scene binary
In its negative wash?
Last Christmas, the first
Christmas after
My father's death, my
Mother still wrapping
The last presents, my son
Off with old friends,
M. stretched out
On the bed of the guest
Room, where we'd thrown
Our things, reading
A biography of Pavlova;
Last Christmas, restless,
Rummaging through a pile
Of old magazines

The semaphores of, flashing yet
In the night: this sequence
Of such languid hieroglyphics —
The corpses of lovers slowly waking
Across that sun-&-sinlit landscape
Of the world's body, calling out
To one another in those songs
By which we name a history, pale
& personal, or otherwise. Still,
It was a careful glance, met
By the vacuum of myth, of
Ourselves blazing
To nothing the way summer mists
Burn off these nearby cliffs,
The way swallows sweep
Into the shifting bodies of clouds
As they rise above the low gorse
& coarse summer thorns. Seven
Turns to me, lips
Lit in the reddish dawn light —
Wild mouth of a fallen poppy —
Ash-scarlet, brash. Naked
Beneath the sky's low dome
Of shadow. Her fingers solemnly
Tunneling my hair, my own mouth
Working the hymn of her ribs.
This is the calming chorus
Of bones, the composed
Sexual languor that so quietly
Resurrects itself, rising
Like a faint down along the length
Of the stirring fern, furred
Blossoms of live lichen blurring
The scarred trunks of the oak.

Stacked beneath the ancient
Blond Magnavox box
Television, I found, quite
Out of nowhere . . . you,
Your voice, that old
Article you'd once done
On Balanchine, its pages
Rippled a little by
The terra infirma stains
Of coffee, or wine —
Your voice
Inked like a strong line
Of hieroglyphs along
The slick waves of the page,
The opened corpse of
The magazine I'd spread
Before me, the echo
Of your voice, the voice
Itself unfolding
Like a body, the serious,
Sly lilt of it — the way
On the phone from
The Hamptons, ten days
Before your death, you said,
"Of course, I'm fine;
Quit worrying about such
Nonsense." Is there
Any other story? Is this
All too obvious, too
Elemental a way
To draw you back into
That room? That same
Elegant voice echoing
Still with all the stories

The sacrament or sacrifice
Of flesh, the architecture of
Our bones like anchors, riven
Beams in the house
Of the body, some doors
Half-closing on what wakes us
Past love. Earth eros, & all
Ages rising. The waves licking
At the unsteady rock of you.

*

Seven like the pulsing lotus
    Of a last emotion
Seven pausing at your open door
    Reaching out a hand
Seven in the fields of white grass
    A suitcase at her side
Seven in her suit of soldier gray
    & untied scarlet scarf
Seven pulling an ebony comb the length
    Of her platinum hair
Seven before the slow particularity
    Of consent
Seven spilling the glass goblet of sand
    Across the body of memory

*

The last parcels of dusk stand
Delivered, again, as each
Simple chord of breath dissolves
In its custom of starlight & eclipse.
I walk with Seven toward the black

You'd tell me sometimes
Over dinner in some dive
In the Village, those
Charmed-life, wild,
& intimately told
Stories;
Of how it would be, of
Course, always &
Simply impossible for
You to choose between a
New Ballanchine ballet
And really anything else,
Including, you admitted
Once, that prized
White elephant of your
Living room, Miss Bishop's
Emerald clavichord! And
So, last Christmas, the first
Christmas after my
Father's death, the smoke
Of the fireplace coiling up
The metal flue, I thought
Of you again
As M. slipped in the video
Cassette of **The Ballerinas,**
The one with Peter Ustinov
As Théophile Gautier,
Gautier introducing one by
One the most
Glamourous dancers of his
Parisian days, each famous
Ballerina (each image:
Historical, gracious, dead)
Danced by Carla Fracci

Château, the juice of winter clover
Still sticky on our hands,
The recitals of fetishes burning
Our tongues. We move off beyond
The murmur of rumor, its perjury
& injury. Those steady jealousies
Consequent of an ancient *Eros Angelus*.
—Christ, I'm so sick of the exemplary,
Those boring & purposeful loves
That lay the angel's glistening head
Along the damp block, & still
Demand we live in that sickening,
Desperate reasonableness of it all —
Whose robes will fall clean tonight?
Only those sealed soberly, finally
In their separate skins, cast
Like bronzes, radiant with loneliness,
The precise gilt of their breath
Rising & falling — brittle curios of death.
No. Spare me; & thrill me with contempt.
Let me walk here quietly, Seven
Yet beside me, the braids of trance
Unraveling as the morning's blue milk
Washes over the low parapets
Of the south tower; beyond us, swirling,
The day blows thick with nettles
& sparrows' sighs. Such is
A residence of angels; fine residue.
Here, into the room Seven's father
Left empty for years, she'd dragged
A wooden table & ancient easel
Up the dry stone stairs, claiming
Its tall, narrow slits of windows
Where she'd sit each spring

As she became miraculously
Incarnate not simply
Of every woman whose body
She inhabited as she
Danced, but, also, of each
Dance itself, each clear
Articulation of time
Through time — every
Body once lost to history
Now danced back
Again along the stage, across
The screen, of our, this
Time . . . And I recalled how
Once you told me
Ballet was the perfected
Eloquence of time, spoken
By the body; time's verses
Voiced by the taut,
Spare measure of a body
Through space, across a
Stage so much less
Casual than the world's.
And you believed,
You said, we were all quite
Simply . . . time —
Not in our separate bodies,
Isolate and fragmented, but
In their movement,
The enacted freedom of
Each step gathering toward
The next, the next, and all
The steps themselves
Gathering into a future
Present

Watching the necks of April iris
Erupt like violet fountains; there,
Where her thin white candles
Left little stitches of wax along
The blank stones of the passageway
As she'd come up late at night
To be alone, at last, her one bodily
Inheritance wrapped around her —
Paper-pale French lace. Such
A sensual disdain, slowly scouring
Her body with half-empty honeycombs,
Giving it that certain luster of lust,
The skin's hungry sheen, the skin's seine
Through which the soul passes,
Those feral gashes in our lives. No balm,
No bane. Nail your body, living crucifix,
To mine. In the cypress, this hush of
Summer rain. (I wanted no one else,
Only the simple solace of her —
To step solitary & naked
Into the body's furnace. There, as
I knelt before her, those pearls
Gathering like white mustard seeds
At each red ridge. Some nights, she'd rub
My body raw with limes, with myrrh,
As in those photos of Egyptian corpses
In that antique album she'd found;
The mask she held to my skull:
Balinese, & painted violently with slashes
Of green, its sneer inlaid with venom,
Outlined with an elaborate, delicate piping
Of black worms.) So if dying flesh damns,
Can then the living flesh redeem?
Yes, she said. Let me show you, though

That each single presence
Slowly grew to apprehend,
In his or her own
Individual dance: for some,
A discreet minuet;
Others, an urgent samba; for
You — that grace of time
Embodied, ballet. Beyond
The curtain, the voices
Murmur and mutter, until
We understand
That in this story,
This spliced continuum
Informed by light, we
Are the flesh of time, just
As the dance is. Today,
At my desk, a poorly
Sanded board propped over
The twin square columns
Of ordinary filing
Cabinets, admiring my
Tall labyrinth of debris,
Abandoned letters & drafts,
I lean back
With a cup of coffee,
Staring at the photos
Hung above my typewriter,
Mostly black-&-white,
One in color, of M. on
Stage, from her days as
A ballerina:
Here, in black costume,
En pointe and stilled;
In these two, partnered

Our guards are sworn to allow
No souvenirs of the pain,
Except those which, in your single body,
You will have no choice but to carry.

＊

Seven like the ever-dilating pupil
    Of a summer midnight
Seven uncurling the cut stilled frames
    Lengths of 16mm film uncoiling
Seven reaching across the burgundy sheets
    Brushing my nipples with rouge
Seven at the edge of her own body
    Where touch sears the stunned air
Seven phoning an old lover in Rio
    Naked in bed her boots still on
Seven standing alongside your idling cab
    Swearing like an evangelist again
Seven like Cervantes' windmill on fire
    The evening of the final harvest
Seven before the torn black starchart on
    The south observatory wall
Seven & her long-blessed trinity of ghosts

＊

It was into these simple spirals
Of exile & neglect
I came to her, like any brother to ash,
My own body's hardened, bloody hinges
Stiff as every abacus of the dead,
The graphs & paths of my nerves
Vague as cumulus. Acres

Through a scene set
In a leafy summer garden;
This last, as Coppelia
Come to life . . .
These images, these images
Of a body frozen
In time, of time frozen
In the shape of a body,
The exquisite line of
The stilled body
Giving the illusion
That it might be rising
Quite on its own
Into the evening air,
Such a momentary
Resurrection, such an
Inevitable assumption
Into the grace
Of the heavens, just as
The ballerina seems
Not even to touch
The earth, for that moment,
And that, until the fluid
Tableaux of her body
Passing before us
In time become a simple
Testimony to
The harmonies of the flesh,
Spirit, and the air . . .
It is the dance, then,
*Which enacts the **being** of*
Time, the dance
Which renders a body
Immaterial. So,

Of smeared butterflies rising
Around me, lifting up from the plaid
Grid of the fields. Bamboo oboes,
Once silent, rehearsing again
The notes of memory's
Marginalia, its little vistas of
Raving regret. On the mahogany table
By her bedside, an old photo
Of her pubis shaved to alabaster, soft
Powder whitening skin like plaster,
A statue sanded slowly to negative
In the light. Those shifting
Borders of the body, near definitions
Erased by time & error, every fluent
Flux of love's denial, & disease —
A carving, hard carving away. It was
At the thin gristle of such a history
We touched the beloved decay, held
In the other's custody —
Turning slowly in the air like swallows,
Stunned quiet as children by
The nude brutal heat of
Our bodies, tongues blunt as
Seeds of crystal quartz. There,
Sheathed by circumstance,
Seven woke: *Touch me* —
The shivering blade of us, small sins,
Melting again the cathedrals of swans
& nectar. The sad choir-song
Of gypsy dogs. A nervous gamecock
Strutting in his wicker cage, screaming
Into the silk pockets of the night. A simple
Convergence of smoke with smoke, timely,
Our own — like violins twined

We are the story, time,
Just as my father's
Body, a few hours
After his death, stretched
Out upon the bed, so
Empty of spirit
It seemed to float there
Like a magician's
Hovering accomplice, just
As he is the story, his body
As stilled as those
Of the corpses
In every grainy photograph
He tore out week
After week from our daily,
Morning newspaper,
All those years of Vietnam,
As his face each week
Grew more grim; as are
Those scrapbooks filled
With articles & photos of
His more than thirty years
As a tennis champ —
Endless, yellowing shots
Freezing his body at the
Exact moment of service,
Reaching for a small globe
Hovering beyond reach,
His body as perfectly
Poised as a dancer's or
Model's at rest,
Held out of time until
That final moment
It gave up all composure,

In the branches of a willow tree, or scrolls
Unrolled along the château's terrace, or
The wall beyond our years being slowly
Inscribed by ivy, by desire.

*

Seven like a glowing thumbprint of ash
    Printed upon my eyelids
Seven at the avant garde concert of clocks
    Webbed by elegant orchestral lies
Seven chalky & indistinct as one of Raphael's
    Final Vatican cartoons

*

Desire remains, earth
Flamed & charged by blood; desire
Remains. The whipped pulp of a body's
Opium, a bud burning in the clay pipe,
Spikes of lamplight piercing
The anxious starling of dream: the room
Rank with sweat, with sex. At last,
The moonlight etching the mirror
Hung beneath the sky's bowed trellis
Sketches the ersatz zero
Of one's own appalling heart. One's,
Meaning my own, as I lean above
The text of Seven's body: her skin
Still the color of fallen apricots,
Nipples no darker than topaz,
The soft tattoo of
Orphan space radiating
From her face. That faintly metallic

Lay brittle as an ancient
Birch-bark canoe set adrift
By the kneeling elders
On those swirling currents
Of the world's river,
To find its own way
Home; just as his body
Is the story . . .
Just as that photograph
Of M. en pointe,
The whole force of her
Endless, delicate
Limbs
Lifting her to the peak
Of ascension, arms
Pointing up to the clouds
Painted on the sky of
The set, just as
She is the story; just as you
Remain the story: your
Voice, you,
Phoning from Tenth Street
To remind me to send up
That new & elegant,
Empty leather address book,
My long-promised
Recompense for — with
What seemed my endless
City-to-city moves
And travels — completely,
You said, "obliterating
The Esses!" It's
Here, that blank
Address book, still;

Taste of her skin; simple resonance.
Such odd physical scriptures
To the oblique. The braille
Of her pain scrawled in half-moons —
Her spine beneath my hand, cool zipper
Of bone. Seven, honing our future
To a single finger of blame, erect stone
Plinth rising above this double tomb.
Ghost stone, I want to be a ceremony —
Still ravenous & carrion before you.
(She dreamt she woke again in Florence,
Living in an essay on *virtù*.) Don't pity
My nerves, unworldly figure of *you*;
The flesh awakened's rarely new. So,
Where is the rapture; who is the raptor?
Ashes in a silver cup, the ravage of these
Carnal quests, & consolations. Bodies
Released again into a predictable pain
Both arrogant & unrestrained,
Daily, & dependable as Cézanne's doubt.
Here, she complained, Take my Swanlute,
& explain how its harp-limbs resonate
With all these catacomb dimensions
Of the burnished heart. Seven,
Poised fiercely as open steel scissors
On the bed, the promise of climax, of
Hades, rivers, & returns — Oh, Baby
Orpheus, she whispered, please come
Take me home; I'll drape us in shades
Of black diamonds. Amazing; there
It was: that same ancient negative
Of the self, empty of space, afloat
Like a white iris on its black mattress,
A singing skull drifting on the world's

Its black, imitation
Ostrich cover
Embossed with a silver
Figure, the silhouette of
A boy skating
Over a frozen lake,
Sketching with the honed
Edges of his skates
The random tracings that
Mirror the warmer, shifting
Currents below — that
Invisible weaving, the pulse
Of the penetrating river.
One evening, coming
Down the steps
Of Lincoln Center, I froze,
Absolutely paralyzed
By some blade
Along my spine; no mugger,
Just a nerve gone wrong,
A bone ajar, I thought,
Maybe simply an aperture
In time, my own odd,
Cold continuum of time . . .
And it's still present
For me, always, this
Present that moves
Through the ever-present
Moment of death,
Extended, slowly bending,
As it is released from
Its final instant, until
It becomes simply the
Flowing element in which

Riverbed. Come closer, Seven said;
Feel the way my lips are soft as
Those fat, reckless bees torn &
Ribboned by sunlight, still hungry,
Still moving through the universe,
Licking those long sapphire hairs
Of God's favorite infant tulips.
Come closer, the world said; & in truth,
I had turned to pull her body to me.

*

Seven holding high the mask of Janus
    To the applause of our friends
Seven undressing in the dawn winter light
    As Pierrot lifts up his icy face
Seven pausing a moment as she descends
    Her glass-&-copper stairway announcing:
Doesn't it seem odd the way the classical
    Always finds a need to return?
Seven like the kaleidoscope of Titian's wings
    Enfolding the corrupted audience
Seven unveiling her violet birthmark
    Of the living Atlantis
Seven turning back in the blinding sheer
    Of a withering final glance
Seven waking alone as the nightingale on
    The unmarked tomb of Orpheus . . .

We forever move, again;
That expanse of loves
We define
With every movement of our
Bodies, every act, every
Choice, every step,
Every voice rising to some
Surface where a familiar
Whipping of wings
Begins to gather, to rise,
Slowly driving the rhythm
Of the air, like echoes
Of the voices claiming us,
The presence of a death
So much our own
It wears a lover's face,
The landscape of the lover's
Worldly body; where even
The sunlight, as they say,
Dances along the water
Of the fountain . . .
Reflecting each exhalation
Of the spirit, every shade
Of communion, the steady
Unfolding angels of breath
Held and, at last, released,
Released finally & softly
As a prayer . . .

Notes

The quotation from Paul Éluard is taken from *Uninterrupted Poetry: Selected Writings of Paul Éluard*, translated by Lloyd Alexander (New Directions, 1975).

The passage from Sidney Keyes can be found in *Sidney Keyes: A Biographical Inquiry*, by John Guenther (London Magazine Editions, 1967).

The quotation from Eugenio Montale comes from his poem "Due nel crepuscolo," from his book *La Bufera e Altro* (Arnoldo Mondadori Editore, 1957). In William Arrowsmith's translation (*The Storm and Other Things*, Norton, 1985), the passage reads:

> And I, overwhelmed
> by the power weighing around us, yield
> to the sorcery of no longer knowing anything
> outside myself . . .

The passage by Pasolini concludes his famous elegy "Le ceneri di Gramsci," from the book of the same title (Aldo Garzanti Editore, 1957). In Norman MacAfee's translation (*Pier Paolo Pasolini: Poems*, Random House, 1982), the passage reads:

> But I with the conscious heart
> of one who can live only in history,
> will I ever again be able to act with pure passion
> when I know our history is over?

The line from Mallarmé is taken from his essay "Hérésies artistiques—l'art pour tous."

The Valéry quotation is from his essay "On Mallarmé," and may be found in this translation by Anthony Bower in *Selected Writings of Paul Valéry* (New Directions, 1950).

Merlin is dedicated to Chichita Calvino.

ABOUT THE AUTHOR

Over the course of his career, David St. John has been honored with many of the most significant prizes for poets, including fellowships from the National Endowment for the Arts and the John Simon Guggenheim Memorial Foundation, the Prix de Rome Fellowship in Literature from the American Academy and Institute of Arts and Letters, and a grant from the Ingram Merrill Foundation. His work has been published in countless literary magazines including *The New Yorker*, *The Paris Review*, *Poetry*, *The American Poetry Review*, *Antaeus*, *Harper's*, and *The New Republic*, and has been widely anthologized. He has taught creative writing at Oberlin College and The Johns Hopkins University, and currently teaches at the University of Southern California. For the past twelve years he has been the poetry editor of *The Antioch Review*.